Emily M Austin

Life Among the Mormons

Emily M Austin

Life Among the Mormons

ISBN/EAN: 9783337029067

Printed in Europe, USA, Canada, Australia, Japan

Cover: Foto ©Lupo / pixelio.de

More available books at **www.hansebooks.com**

Emily M Austin

Life Among the Mormons

ISBN/EAN: 9783337029067

Printed in Europe, USA, Canada, Australia, Japan

Cover: Foto ©Lupo / pixelio.de

More available books at **www.hansebooks.com**

MORMONISM;

OR,

LIFE AMONG THE MORMONS

—BY—

EMILY M. AUSTIN,

BEING AN AUTOBIOGRAPHICAL SKETCH; INCLUDING AN
EXPERIENCE OF FOURTEEN YEARS OF
MORMON LIFE.

MADISON, WIS.
M. J. CANTWELL, BOOK AND JOB PRINTER, KING ST.
1882.

PREFACE.

To those who read this narrative, I will say, no flowery words will accompany these pages; and, as it is a true story, I trust it will meet the approval as also the common good of all. Feeling my incapability of doing literary work, I hope to be generously pardoned for all mistakes, both in form and in language, of this little history; hoping to furnish something which the reader never would have had without the earnest perseverance of the author; the benefits of which, I believe, will prove to be of value to all who peruse this volume carefully. There are disinterested persons who have advised me and even urged that I should write my experience—those in whom I have the utmost confidence and regard, and who have had some knowledge of my former experience; and through their repeated requests, I have finally decided to give this work to the public, hoping my efforts will meet with their approbation.

I have devoted much time and, I may say, unlimited attention to accomplish this task, in view of giving an accurate account in the historical part, the circumstances of which have occurred within my own knowledge; and carefully observing to found all goodness in religious principles. Some people probably may tnink that that should have been excluded, but I know with whom I have to deal; and I hope I may thus allure those thoughtless creatures to higher things. Add to this, some of my acquaintances or wordly friends, are afraid I shall be too Methodistical, a term which is applied to vital Christianity. In that kind of prudence, there is but little safety. May I therefore be strenghtened by Him who is able to make us wise, and may we increase in knowledge through Christ our living head.

INTRODUCTION.

Keeping a hotel at the foot of the Alleghany mountains as early as the year 1813, was not a very easy task, as there were no railroads, all transportation of merchandise was conveyed by four-horse teams, and all cooking done in fire-places, and to hear teams coming down the steep mountains in the dead hours of night with that continual "paddy whep," "paddy whep, whey," this was not a morphine to sleep by, but on the contrary; every member of the house was up making preparations for a hungry crowd of Pennsylvania teamsters. My father's family were the only New York people in that vicinity, and we never learned the dialect of the Pennsylvanians. The people were hardy and very industrious, and in many respects, obliging. Our house was conducted in quietness, and I believe, prosperiety crowned our most sanguine wishes consistent with the view of making money. Nevertheless there were things to be considered beyond the chance of gain, and in view of the class of people with whom our associations were immediately concerned, also in view of many co-operative motives, the minds of our parents agreed as one to make our stay as limited as possible in that locality. However, two or three years elapsed before a removal could be made without a great sacrifice. The prospects, too, were flattering. Finding it a matter to be duly considered, and whether it was not better to make the sacrifice and remain a few years longer at least, was the question. With a view of pecuniary advantages, the latter suggestion predominated. But the situation was not in anywise adapted to the taste of my parents. My father's previous avocation, that of music-teaching, had in former years been attended with success. Not so in keeping a boarding house. While at this we had much hurry and bustle; we had critical and fastidious people to please, and, in many instances, we were somewhat baffled to know how to gain that point.

Five years had now passed and our home was no longer at the Mountain House, but a far happier home on the Unadilla river, in the state of New York. The birds sang sweetly in the trees on the river bank and in the bright sunlight, and welcomed us from the shade of mountain life, into a more congenial clime.

My brothers and sisters all seemed to enjoy the sunlight away from the mountain, amid birds and flowers, and a clear purling river at the lower part of our garden. I had at this time four sisters and two brothers, and a more lively family was never reared by parents, take the world over. Our mother was the daughter of Colonel Lyon, a distinguished officer in the war of 1812; he was also in high standing in the Masonic lodge, and was counted one of the first in the most tender regards and affections of good society. It is needful also to say that our father was one of the foremost in the same lodge and in society. Colonel Lyon was one of the first settlers in Chenango county, N. Y. The city now called Oxford was then known as Lyon's settlement. Two or three of his brothers were with him in this Indian forest, and they were the only white men within seventy miles. Lyon and his brothers were Indian traders, and for several years this was their constant business. Their buildings were logs, the roofs and floors of bark; the fireplaces, the roots of trees. In this border home, with his brothers settled around him, no man could be more happy then he. They were fortunate in getting shipment for the abundant choice furs which they purchased of the Indians for very small sums, and for which they received large pay; and, eventually, they became wealthy. Emigration now began to pour in, and the place became settled with white inhabitants. It was about this time the war of 1812 commenced, and Thomas Lyon was one of the first who enlisted, being a bold, courageous soldier. He was soon promoted to office and afterward became colonel of a regiment. His regiment, with several others, was sent to Canada, where he lost his life by the explosion of a magazine; an act of the British; hundreds were swept into eternity at that instant.

The sword of Colonel Lyon was all they ever obtained. This had his name in silver letters upon the hilt; his mahogany casket and grave clothes and sword were sent to his family in New York, and his death was commemorated as one who had laid down his useful life for his country. His casket was followed to the place of interment accompanied with a band of music, he was buried with the honors of war, and by the Masonic order. I am proud to see his name recorded in the United States history; furthermore, to know I am a grand-daughter of so bold a patriot; and, although his mortality is oblivious, his name still lives.

LIFE AMONG THE MORMONS.

CHAPTER I.

I am willing that my readers should know something of my ancestry, for reasons which may be followed with good results, both for the reader as also the writer; furthermore, it is necessary for particular reasons that my readers should, in a compact form, know something of our beginning, as it measurably shows the probability, or the possibility, of people who are ever so well protected and reared, of the monster breaking the walls, and error entering in and taking the place of truth and uprightness. We are constantly traveling in slippery paths, in which the utmost watchfulness and care should be taken to keep our feet from the snares of the fowler.

After making these few preliminary remarks, I will proceed. The voice of music was now apparent, in fact, in the days of which I am writing, we knew of no time that our father had not lessons in music to give; thus his time was taken up away from home. I have sometimes accused my father of partiality, as he taught the eldest of our family the rules of singing and never taught the younger ones; finely, to free my mind, I said, "father, why do you not learn us the rules of singing?" "It is because," said he "you have natural voices and you know what time is, if you wish to learn to play on the instrument I will teach you." Our mother was a very good woman and very careful and industrious, as we used to say when she told us how terribly she disliked to see so many little fingers idle; so she hired a lady in the house to learn us to braid straw. It was not the common kind of braiding, but the manufacturing fine braid for bonnets; we also learned to make gimp and all kinds of straw trimmings, which was at this time and for many years after, very fashionable, and there were many large manufactories in this business. The gimp was not as tedious to learn as we had anticipated. We readily learned this, also making all patterns and designs. The style and fashion made the demand more than we could fill. We were not the only ones who engaged in this, however, there were many who made fortunes at this beautiful work of art. Our father, not being satisfied with his salary, went to Canada to try his fortune in teaching; his income being far less than what he considered worth the time and attention which he performed. Deeming this his duty, he left for a far better prospect in the future. After telling us he would not return empty handed, we bade him farewell; and, after he had shaken our little hands and kissed us good bye, he departed.

Allured by the sallies of youth we sprang to each duty as an enjoyment, filling up the measure of our days in an enjoyment of the fanciful, or the realities and practical events, of our happy existence; each one of us falling in the ranks of social plays, whether theatrical or that which the eldest of our circle suggested. But now the separation of two of our sisters was considered by us unbearable. Our mother being over-persuaded by a lady friend to let them go into families who had no daughters, they were adopted as their own; thinking, probably, that we had more than our share of girls, but we children could not be persuaded that we had any to spare; there were only five, and now we had but three. This reminds me of a family in the east. They were farmers and had nine boys. Their farm was productive (which indeed it should be) and yielded abundance of large potatoes. One day the youngest of the nine, feeling a keen demand of appetite, went slily, and getting a large number of potatoes covered them up in a bed of hot coals in the mammoth fireplace, which served for roasting potatoes as well as every other kind of cooking. He then went out to his work thinking of the feast when those potatoes were done. After working for an hour he returned, and on examining the pile he began to think it did not look as large as when he left them, yet he had one advantage; his lower limbs were far more than ordinary length, and he would soon find out how many he had. Fortunately he could work more handy for being tall; he therefore began to poke, and, and fining himself *minus,* he began to cry and started to find his mother who was in the cheese house. He made long strides to where she was working and bawled out — "Mother, the boys have got most all my potatoes; I haint got but fourteen left." "Yes," she said, "and they will get the remaining part too, if you don't hurry back." The boy ran.

CHAPTER II.

I will proceed with my story. I can truly say we missed our sisters. It is a feast for sisters to be in each others society while in the spring time of life. Allow me to say furthermore if parents knew or could realize the tender union which often exists between children, it is my candid opinion they would, in all probability, use more caution in breaking that union. My sister who was two years younger than myself, was my only messmate; neither did I take her as a substitute for those who had left home. Our spirits were always congenial to each other from the cradle up to old age. In fact, I can say truly, that a more united band of brothers and sisters were never reared. We knew nothing of quarels or disputes in our father's family. I have many times thought of Paul's words, "Be ye kind one to another, tender hearted, forgiving one another even as God for Christ's sake hath forgiven you."

CHAPTER III.

The sudden illness of our sister caused silence to reign in our cottage; and the quietness, together with the monotony of straw braiding, at times became irksome. Then a stroll in woodland was cool and refreshing, on a summer day, to listen to the sweet songsters of the forest. Thus we beguiled the long lonely hours, talking the while of our two sisters' departure from home, and how sad and lonely we had been since they left us. We traversed the hills in search of the wintergreen, which in some places along the hillside, grew plentifully, with their red berries; and we culled the wild roses which came within our reach, and wandered over rough places in search of the squawberries, which grew under the dry foliage. We thus wandered on, insensible of home duties, until we were weary; and sleep, insensibly, stole upon us. We we were now in dreamland among the fairies; and I wonder the robin did not cover us over with leaves, we so much resembled the babes in the woods; now forgetful of home and our sister, who was ill, our mother and brothers, the scenes on the river, the memory of which draws my mind back through mist of time to covet the moments we were enjoying then.

Who will not say that childhood and youth were the happiest period of their life? At that time the ills of our existence were not visible.

CHAPTER IV.

We awoke. A robin is on a limb near us with a worm in his mouth. We jump from our summer day's retreat, and turn our feet homeward. "Dear mother," said my sister Jane, as we entered the cottage, "we have been asleep in the woods and a robin came and waked us; what did you think had become of us, mother?" "O, I hardly know what I thought," said she. "I supposed you were in the shade somewhere." "How is sister? has the doctor been to see her?" I asked. "Yes, my child, and his countenance tells of what he thinks is approaching rapidly."

CHAPTER V.

Day after day we watchfully stood by her bed; and, when night came, we did not slacken our vigilance. One only had to behold her, to pronounce her past the skill of any one, on this earth, to cure. Our friends and neighbors were attentive, all seeming to show a kindly, helping hand and a sympathizing heart. One bright morning, as the sun was shining through the window shutters, we asked her if the sun did not hurt her eyes. "O, no," she said, "I love it;" and began to sing the words,

> "Refreshing showers of grace divine,
> From Jesus flows to every vine,
> Which makes the dead revive."

We were now convinced that her stay was not with us; but, when the doctor visited her in the evening, he was pleased to find her better. Slowly she began to regain her strength, and fourteen weeks, to a day, found her again on her feet. We could now attend our Sabbath school and church which we had been deprived of so long; and, feeling ourselves at liberty, we rejoiced in our sister's recovery, and in again joining our class in Sabbath school.

After this our eldest brother went to a trade with our uncle, who lived in the town of Guilford, Chenango county. He was to stay until twenty-one; and now only four of us children remained at home. Our time was taken up in going to school, and straw work; and our clean blue and white checked aprons never made an apology for our doing otherwise, for they always seemed to be ready and laid out where we could see them plainly. "We must see Esquire, Lacy," said mother one morning as we sat at the breakfast table, "you must go this afternoon," mother said to our brother Morris." "What have you reference to, mother?" said Morris, sitting back in his chair and looking inquiringly, and at the same time patting little Mink on the head; "to see if any of your father's scholars have left any more money for us, as they promised. I have been looking for a letter, but I cannot wait much longer. It is the first of September, and we have had only two or three payments from that school. I have had to pay the family doctor, and now I am short again; I put ten into the treasury box and intend to keep it their, at least as long as I can." "O, that will do," said mother in response to my brother; "we must learn something of rural economy," continued mother, "this is a profitable lesson to learn, my son, and the sooner we learn it the better, what do you say at that?" "I say

> I wonder not, things have been,
> 'Tis clear enough to any;
> The few alone can be rich,
> The poor must be many.
>
> And who can wonder at the state
> Of being blue or jolly;
> Dame nature, on her page of faje.
> Writes fun or melancholy.

CHAPTER VI.

"Come, that will answer," said mother, as she removed the table cloth from the little neat breakfast table. "Suppose you harness the ponies and take me with you sister," Sarah said, "a ride in our easy carriage will, I am sure, help me much; and it's been so long since I saw town." They were soon off and had passed behind the hill a little ways from the river leading to the villa. Our home here was picturesque, with the road running past the cottage and a hill jutting out just below us, which made a curve, or a circle, for teams to pass between that and the river. The hill was covered with laurel, which in the spring of the year sent out its fragrance from its blossoms. The woods were not very far from our cottage, just back a little from the upper part of our garden; shrubbery was of a choice cultivation, consisting of several varieties of rose trees and many other very choice and delicious forms of shrubs. This place was made still more picturesque by a view from the opposite side of the river, as building was in progress of almost every kind; mills, in a particular manner, were in rapid progress, and the level green and the rocks and hills made the scenery still more beautiful. A large porch was in front of our cottage; and in summer we spent many pleasant evenings enjoying the cool, refreshing breeze from the river, and listening to the whippoorwill. We received letters from our father time after time, and as often received money. We had now advanced a considerable in means, our income was not large, however; we were satisfied with the expectation that our father would bring home considerable money. We were mindful of the promise he made on leaving home, that he should not come empty-handed. We spent months and years, in the anticipation of happier times to come, yet how could we wish more happiness than that which we already enjoyed. Was it not enough that we could crowd in among roses, double roses, June roses, pink roses wet with the dew of heaven, our morning resort? Yes, and to hear the sweet singing of birds, names unknown to us then! Our happy home on the river of Unadilla, Unadilla village almost within hailing distance; friends and companions crowded our pathway as we journied onward in life's thoroughfare, intermingling golden threads of joy and happiness.

God was good to us then, although we did not realize it; we knew of a Majesty, a Great Ruler of the universe; yet we had not thought of loving him, knew too, or at least had been taught that he made all things; and we picked flowers to inspect the magnificent handiwork of our Creator, and it was wonderful. We loved his work, and the author we could not see. We imagined He must be a beautiful being, as we scrutinized the soft petals of the rose and other flowers, the vines, the woodbine and jasamine, clinging to the lattice of the porch. We touched the petals of flowers to our cheeks; the touch was soft and velvety, and we thought, who but a lovely being could give to us such riches. We looked up to the sky as the shade of night had gathered over us, and there, we too, beheld the work of His hands; the stars, radiant with glittering brightness, and wondered if such a God was mindful of us.

CHAPTER VII.

Our elder brother visited us four times a year. He came to see us and stayed three days every visit. Our uncle, whose name was Samuel Mills, lived in the town of Guilford, Chenango county, New York. Here my brother served three years apprenticeship at the tanners trade. Our uncle had several sons. It may be needful to mention their names, some of them at least. The first Wilcox; second, Samuel; third, Simeon; fourth, Harvey. These were the only ones I remember, but there were several more, and a number of daughters. Uncle Sam, as we called him, was a strictly business man, and at the time of which I am writing, had a large dairy, and always (I mean in the summer) made abundance of cheese and butter from forty cows He also had a large tannery and boot and shoe shop. My brother remained there. I think at the time I have spoken of his visit, he had accomplished half of his time; and now as our brother had come, we must all join in to make his stay as agreeable as possible. So one afternoon as mother was on business away from home, and being detained until dark — we were conversant with nearly all the plays in vogue, and were in the height of their merits — when a loud rap at the front door startled us, and springing, we opened the door. A gentlemen stepped in, removing his hat, he enquired: "Does Mrs. C. live here," when answered in the affirmative, he then asked if she was at home. The voice was our fathers, but we could not designate his countenance as a half partition across the large front room shut the light from his face. "She will come presently," said my brother, "please be seated." He readily accepted the chair offered, when our mother came in. On entering she glanced at the stranger. She flew to his arms, and pronouncing his name, says: "Is this my husband?" "Is this the woman I call my wife," was the response. By this time we were all around him. We were all glad indeed to see him safe from a far country. It had been a little over three years he had been away from home. We were all happy in his embrace once more. We were twice glad when father took from his portmanteau a bag, and on untying the string, he filled mothers lap full of gold and silver. "This is too heavy for me too handle," said mother, dipping it into the leather sack with her hand. "O! see the gold," says one. "How pretty it is," says another. "I wonder you were not robbed," said another. "We will put this away," said father, "or we may get rid of it sooner than we like. We will lock it up in the secretary, that will be a safe place." We soon arranged supper, enjoying a comfortable repast once more with our father's presence at the head of the table. "My thoughts have been on coming home for some time, especially when I learned of Sarah's illness, until you wrote me of her recovery, having a great deal to do at the time of her illness it was an impossibility to leave at that time; however she looks well now, and you are all looking remarkably well," taking out his handkerchief to wipe off a greatful tear. "Yes, all is well that ends well," said our mother. "Esick will soon, or within a few months, finish his trade, and then I intend going to a better place than this, I shall buy a farm probably." "O, I hope you wont think best to wait until his time is out, dear papa," said sister Sarah, "we can go onto a farm without him. He will not be a farmer any more than papa is, will you brother?" "No," said Esick, as he took up father's hat and put it on his own head; we all laughed heartily, for he looked altogether too small for such a hat.

Our brother, Esick Lyon, was a small, young man, only a little over five feet in height. He was also of a slender form. Our father was fleshy and rudy, light, curly hair, blue eyes, which were large and expressive, his forehead high and white; he was not tall, but of medium height. I have now given a description of some of our family, it is not needful to say more on this subject.

CHAPTER VIII.

Six months had passed, which found us on a farm in the township of Greene, after bidding farewell to our cottage home, on that beautiful river the Unadilla. Here life opened out altogether different from what we had been accustomed to. However we managed to depicture the farmer in the opening, leaving the view of success equivocal; although our father availed himself of all the useful information attainable, as to the best plan of arranging things in such a manner as to make it profitable. Remote from the advantages we had hitherto enjoyed, shut out from the world in view of benefits, which were uncertain, we knew the only way was to solace ourselves with the thought that our parents would, after a few years, get a dislike to that way of living. It is true we were situated pleasantly; the farm was productive, and one of father's brothers opened a farm joining us. He was a magistrate, and often had other business to attend to, which called his attention away from home a great part of the time. Our father, too, had besettings from every town around us; for teaching, however, he managed this to the best advantage, having his schools the nearest home possible, the eldest members of the family attending with him, sometimes accompanied by our uncle H. M. C.

As I have already taken up too much time with the story of our beginning, I will endeavor to make this as limited as possible, as nothing of importance transpired, excepting the death of a dear little sister, the memory of which left its pang on all of our hearts. Subsequently our father, and our uncle, sold their farms for a good round sum, and bought a residence in the pleasant town of Guilford, Chenango county, New York. Our brother's time had been long expired, yet he still remained as a journeyman with Uncle Mills, and suiting his action to his words, that "practice makes perfect."

"Now what?" said mother, as brother Esick came in one very fine evening and smiling pleasantly; "any good news? I see you are looking happy." "Yes, mother," he said, "where is sister?" taking off his hat and seating himself near to us. Jane turned, and said she could guess what was up. "Then you think you can guess, do you, little pet?" well, guess once, "no, I shan't; but I know all the same. I don't tell all I know in one breath." "There, lass," said brother, patting her curls with the tip of his fingers, "run and tell Sarah I wish to see her immediately; run quick please." Sarah came all out of breath, enquiringly putting her ear close to brother's face to hear the secret, for Jane told her it was 'twas a great secret. "Are you crazy, or what?" said brother Esick Lyon, as he arose, and putting his arm around her waist, and quietly dancing a light French step, no he said "its no secret, I only wish you to accompany me to a social party, now sister put on style, there's a very nice young lady going to be there, and I hear she is from Philadelphia, too. O, where's my trunk, ma?" he said, as he made up an awful face, and at the same time staggering like a drunken man, and in the performance hitched his toe and upset mother, but she was taken up as soon as she was taken down, and here the play was ended. I never saw my sister look prettier. She was dressed in blue silk, trimmed with white lace, a gold chain and watch, with a pink rose in her light auburn hair, which inclined to curl, always bright and wavy. My brother, too, was dressed in black broadcloth, a gold watch and a French necktie, looking extremely well. The coach came, and they disappeard through the hall door. As they passed out, mother looked at us and smiled, as only mothers can, and then a proud look passed over her countenance; proud of her children, as only mothers are. We need not ask how they enjoyed the evening, their countenance plainly told.

My brother was delighted with Miss Jewel; and more than one looked upon Esick Lyon with a suspicious, jealous eye, whenever their observation found them together; and it was not my brother's or Miss Jewel's intention to render the circumstances of this case more equal, as far as this concerned them, they both agreed to relinquish etiquette for a time and adopt obsolete custom. This was undoubtedly their privilege, for they were lovers at first sight. There were presumptious remarks made by the young people, both male and female. In fact one young lady remarked to Esick Lyon that she had the first claim and also she had the staff in her own hands. "Ah," said my brother, "you forget that through politeness a young man often compliments a young lady without the least motive of making her his wife." "Esick Lyon you have made your choice, probably, but let me say to you, that Miss Jewel shall never marry you, never! never! that is, if I can hinder it. Probably she will finish her visit at Deacon Jewel's and then return to Philadelphia, and that will end the courtship between you. Another thing is, she is a milliner, and knows nothing of housekeeping, and her complexion shows that she is entirely and universally unacquainted with a rural or domestic life, and now what do you want of a city lady? asked Lucinda Hartwell, as she took her handkerchief to dry a falling tear. An interruption caused them to be silent for a moment, then Esick Lyon replied, "Miss Jewel is of a good, respectable family; no one can say aught of her. Add to this, her relatives, the Jewels here whom she is visiting, are the very bone and sinew of society in this town; this you know. Furthermore, we are engaged." "Then you and I will exchange gifts, or keepsakes, will we not?" asked Lucinda, as she arose, giving a look of sarcasm, and turning to Esick Lyon to receive the answer. "Suit yourself," was the answer, and all he could say in regard to her inquiry. The presents were returned, and not many weeks had expired before a wedding was announced, and a cordial invitation was given out by the Rev. Mr. Donelson, the pastor of the Presbyterian church in Gilford. The house was crowded to the utmost, from the entry to the gallery. The large organ opened the service; the minister came down from the pulpit; the bridal party advanced, and the solemn ceremony was said in the presence of several hundred persons. Now after all the ceremony was accomplished, and a wedding trip to the great metropolis of the state of Pennsylyania *via* New York had been made; and this was among the things which have been, they, looking forward for things to come, quietly settled down in a snug little home of their own; each one resuming his or her accustomed avocation.

At this time I was desired to go and assist my brother's wife; she wanted me as an apprentice girl, as she was running a large millinery establishment; and eventually I was one among a number of girls, learning the millinery, with a proprietor at the head. Two years had elapsed; at this time my sister had married and lived in the town of Colesville, Broom county, New York. Her husband's name was Newel Knight. He was a staunch Universalist, and his father, Joseph Knight, was also of the same belief. Sister Sarah was of the Presbyterian faith. However, I never knew of any argument between them concerning their religious views. I was now just entering my third year at my brother's, and a revival of religion commenced in the Presbyterian church, and many were exhibiting a great interest in forming a new and more useful life; and I found myself one of that happy number.

During this revival, many were brought to see that the blood of Christ was sufficient to cleanse them from all sin; and I felt an assurance that I was also adopted into the family of God, through his blood. I was now, as I considered — and in fact it was my most earnest wish — to lay aside selfish longings, and look a little to the comfort and good of others. It is true I now had, at an early age, learned a trade; and choosing not to eat the bread of idleness, and furthermore to let independence be my aim, and ever look upon avarice as my worst foe, I felt determined to start out in the right path in pursuing the journey of life. To emulate the example of the good Samaritan effectually, one must be in possession of an independence.

My brother Esick Lyon lived in Pennsylvania, in the town of Sandford, Crawford county. I still remained with them, only making occasional visits at my fathers, in Guilford, and at Colesville; and it was optional with me where to commence when I snould arrive at an age sufficient to do business for myself.

CHAPTER IX.

Six months had elapsed, and we hear a rumor going around that Joe Smith, of whom we had often heard as a fortune teller, was at this time in Colesville, preaching a very strange doctrine, and that our sister and her husband were attentive listeners to his fanaticism. This rumor staggered our wits to comprehend. The story was repeated in our ears almost daily. We knew this same Joe Smith had often been in Colesville, to visit his Universalist friends or brethren. I had seen him two or three times, while visiting at my sisters, but did not think it worth my while to take any notice of him. I never spoke to him, for he was a total stranger to me. However, I thought him odd looking and queer. He also told his friends that he could see money in pots, under the ground. He pretended to foretell people's future destiny, and, according to his prognostication, his friends agreed to suspend their avocations and dig for the treasures, which were hidden in the earth; a great share of which, he said, was on Joseph Knight's farm.

Old Uncle Joe, as we called him, was a wool carder, and a farmer; yet he abandoned all business, and joined with a number of others, to dig for money on his premises. While I was visiting my sister, we have walked out to see the places where they had dug for money, and laughed to think of the absurdity of any people having common intellect to indulge in such a thought or action. However, all of those things had long since become oblivious; for in the time of their digging for money and not finding it attainable, Joe Smith told them there was a charm on the pots of money, and if some animal was killed and the blood sprinkled around the place, then they could get it. So they killed a dog, and tried this method of obtaining the precious metal; but again money was scarce in those diggings. Still, they dug and dug, but never came to the precious treasure. Alas! how vivid was the expectation when the blood of poor Tray was used to take off the charm, and after all to find their mistake, that it did not speak better things than that of Abel. And now they were obliged to give up in despair, and Joseph went home again to his father's, in Palmyra.

Some months after this fruitless enterprise he was married to Miss Emma Hale, a school teacher, a fine girl, of good repute and respectable, though poor parentage. It was at this time, which I have mentioned previously, that the rumor was in circulation concerning the strange doctrine which he was setting forth; and which, indeed, was creating quite a stir among the people, and it surprised us to hear of his return to Colesville with his wife, to meet again with his old money diggers. But now he had entered upon a new project. He declared an angel had appeared to him and told him of golden plates, which were hidden up to come forth on a certain day; and also that the plates were sacred, containing a history of a people who inhabited this continent in ancient days; also it was that which Isaiah the prophet had spoken of; a vision which should become as the words of a book that is sealed; which was delivered to one that was learned, saying: "Read this, I pray thee;" and he said, "I cannot, for it is sealed;" and the book is delivered to one that is unlearned, saying: "Read this, I pray thee;" and he said, "I cannot, for I am unlearned; moreover, inasmuch as this people draw near me, with their mouths and with their lips do honor me, therefore I will proceed to do a marvelous work and a wonder; for the wisdom of their wise men shall perish, and the understanding of their prudent men shall be hid."

This is what was circulated throughout the country, and this is the rumor which was now afloat. Smith brought up many prophecies to show that the Lord was about to do a marvelous work in the last days. He also affirmed that he had seen the angel, and had talked with him face to face; and the angel told him at a certain time he would conduct him to the place where the plates could be obtained; also that he was a chosen vessel in the hands of God, to translate them, and bring them to the world. All this was heard and believed by a large number of persons in Colesville, among whom was my own dear sister and her husband.

Onward hastened the time. The book was translated from the golden plates; it was called the Book of Mormon. Witnesses set their names to the book, testifying that they had seen the plates, and had handled them with their hands; also that they had the appearance of gold. Names of the witnesses: Oliver Cowdry, David Whitmer, Peter Whitmer. Finally, the books were sent out to a wondering people, and many believed in the new doctrine; some of undisputable respectability, taking in both rich and poor. On learning of our sister's conversion into this faith, we were doubtful as to the accuracy of the report; also believing her to be of an unshaken mind and principle, we therefore consoled ourselves with the thought of this being a probable mistake. At this time they had organized a church, which consisted of sixty members. They were also at the commencement baptizing and confirming by the laying on of hands, for the reception of the Holy Ghost. The same ordinance also was practiced to heal the sick and cast out devils; all of which was accomplished by the laying on of the hands of the ordained elders of the Church of Latter Day Saints.

I now visited my sister to try if possible to convince her of the error into which she had innocently been decoyed and deceived. However, this was of no effect whatever. She was as firm as the everlasting hills in the belief of Mormonism, and seemed to have the whole Bible at her tongue's end. She was of the belief that God had again visited His people, and again set His hand, the second time, to recover the house of Israel. She also was of the belief that this was the work, and warned me against condemning that which I did not understand, lest I should be found fighting against God's will.

By this time my faith had grown weak in regard to changing her mind, and I thought it best for me to go back to my brother's, and henceforth to let them alone. I considered it a deception and delusion; but as I was necessarily detained over the Sabbath, I attended services with my sister. The discourse was delivered by Oliver Cowdry, an elder of the Mormon church, and a witness to the gold plates. After preaching, several were baptized, and the converts were increasing rapidly. For some time, having meetings daily, and also evenings, the excitement was great, insomuch that many were overcome by the spirit, and were, seemingly, unconscious of all around them. On awaking from this trance, they would say they were happy, and had seen angels and talked with them. However, I did not feel interested in this direction. It had hitherto appeared most simple of all things, and I was decidedly against such proceedings. I was still detained at my sister's. For some reason I could not get back to my brother's, in Sandford; and, at this time, I cannot remember the cause of my prolonged stay. While I tarried I attended church with my sister. Sidney Rigdon came into Colesville any preached to a numerous congregation. We did not class him as a Mormon, as we were informed that he was a Baptist minister, from Paynsville, Ohio. The words of his text — "O, foolish Gallatians, who hath bewitched you that ye should not obey the truth?" It was, indeed interesting, and great attention and silence prevailed; and it was acknowledged by all to be the best sermon ever preached in that vicinity. He stayed several days, seeming to have special business with Joseph Smith and the leaders of the new Mormon church. I mention these facts only because I think to this day that he had something to do in getting up the

Book of Mormon, and we found, after his return to Ohio, that he was also a believer in the new doctrine.

This seemed rather strange, that a man of his talents should be a believer in anything so strange as this appeared to be; and, as I was now about to go back to my brother's in Sandford, my sister told me that God would give me a sure witness to the truth of this work, if I would only ask him; it was my custom to daily go to him. I therefore thought to make this an item to be remembered, and, in my feeble petition I humbly asked Him to show me the truth of this, least I should be found to rebel against His holy will. I had selected a retired place in the grove, and an incident occurred which is to this day beyond my comprehension. It was three loud raps on a tree near me; so loud, and in quick succession, that I felt the jar and wind of the blows. I immediately arose to my feet and closely examined the place. All was silent, and nothing could be seen. I was somewhat frightened, and never thought of this as a witness to the truth of Mormonism. The excitement had now reached to a high pitch; and the old father of all mischief and disturbance, helped to circulate a report that I was intending to join the Mormon church on the

Sabbath following. This false rumor reached the attention of my brother, and the church of which I was a member. A complaint was entered against me to the church; next, a course of gospel labor commenced. They visited me three times; each time I assured them I had no thought of joining them (the Mormons). This they did not seem to hear; and, to sum up the matter, their uncharitable actions drove me farther and still farther from believing in anything good. I was not yet eighteen years of age. My heart was stricken, and I could see no love manifested. In the advancement of time I perceived they still believed I intended joining that church, without listening to what I told them or trying to ascertain the truth in regard to it. They did not come to me in love and ask me to go with them to my brother's or my father's, but continued to come and see me. I had been homesick, and had had several hearty crying spells in secret, because I could not get back to my brothers. The team was always in use, or some other very essential thing to attend to. I acknowledge my feelings were not as pleasant as they probably might have been had I been situated in a more pleasing, cheerful, delightful attitude.

It was one Sabbath day, beautiful and

and bright. We had been to church. Several had assembled at Newell Knight's, as was the general custom, for he was an elder. A message was sent to me that Esick Lyon wished to see me at the grove, which was some distance from the house; that he wished a friendly interview with me. I felt reluctant in granting his request, but through the advice of my sister I ventured to go. I at this time attempted to make plain to him the reason of my tarrying at my sister's, and I then believed he understood me perfectly. While in the midst of our conversation, who should come but the Rev. Mr. Sherer, pastor of our church in Sandford. He came and took my hand, and holding it so long and firmly I thought it odd. I had tried to disengage this unwelcome cordiality, but had no success. I then asked my brother's assistance; but he declined, saying I would do well to listen to Mr. Sherer's council. However, we were not in the least surprised to find every member of the Mormon church on hand. My sister hastened to me, and soon wrenched off the hand that held mine. "What are you doing with my sister?" she asked with an authoritative expression. "What are you doing with my sister?" again she asked, her face looking white as snow as she uttered these words.

There were about sixty Mormons now in close contest with my brother and Mr. Sherer. I left them to settle the matter as best they could; I cared not how if I only obtained my liberty. I then enjoyed a few moments of sweet, uninterrupted tranquility, having the house to myself for at least one half hour. This might probably have been a little skirmish in the christian warfare; but if this is the case, O, tell it not in Gath.

The members of the household were gathered in again from the field of strife, together with quite a number of elders, and also members, and were once more seated composedly, talking and singing, when my uncle rode up to the door on a white, stately, beautiful horse, and as he drew up he exclaimed, "You are happy now you have accomplished your purpose, and I hope you enjoy it; but this will not be of long endurance, let me tell you." "O, yes," said one of the elders, "you are an attorney, probably you will take steps in this matter, but not to-day." Sir," said another Mormon elder, "you are mad; you look as white as the horse you are riding; to-day is the holy Sabbath, and you are a deacon; don't indulge in such a passion." Many hard words were used on both sides; and here the subject ended, by putting spurs to the white steed, under a two hundred and twenty burden, which seemed light and easy for the noble animal. That night was dark and rainy. A messenger was plodding through darkness, mud and rain, and dead of night, to my father's in Guilford, thirty miles distant. The messenger said he did not spare the horse. He arrived at Guilford some time in the night, and, waking them, told the story. Afer getting permission, he went to a lawyer and obtained a power of attorney. Arriving at Colesville, he came to me saying he now had authority to take me away. I told him "I could go without all that trouble, and did not think it necessary to use the law in the case; and now, as I have a good opportunity, I will speak a few words for myself — this was my brother-in-law, whom I will call P—— T——. Probably you are somewhat unacquainted with the aflair altogether; I will say, that I came here for the purpose of talking with my sister about the absurdity of believing in Mormonism, and finding it useless to say more on that subject, I concluded to return to my brother, Esick Lyon, and let her enjoy her own opinion. But Newell Knight was busy, and could not spare the time or the team either to take me home, and he desired me to tarry a few days, he would then go with me.

"Not long after this it was circulated that I intended to go into the Mormon church, and a copy of the complaint which was entered against me to the church in Sandford, was handed me. It read as follows:

"*To the Church of Christ, in Sandford:*

"WHEREAS, E. M., a member of said church, embraces a most wicked and dangerous heresy; and whereas, we have taken with her the first and second steps of gospel labor, without obtaining satisfaction, we therefore make complaint to the church of which said E. M. is a member, praying that the brethren of said church would bring her to an account for her unchristian conduct; and, as in duty bound, your servants will ever pray. H. M.
E. L.
B. S."

"Those are the names of the officers in our church who signed this copy of complaint. And now you are here with authority to take me away. What does all this bustle signify? Explain to me, if you can? It is all plain to me; I am willing, yes, more than willing, to go back to my brother's." "Can you go to-morrow?" asked P—— T——. "I can go to-day, if you like," I answered; "but let me ask, what did you understand in this affair? Probably you understood that I was obstinate in this matter, did you not?" "I did," said P—— T——, "and I believe what you have stated to be true as gospel. I also know who the instigator is, but I shall decline telling at present, for certain reasons." "I know who you allude to, but it would not be proper to mention his name; the church have great confidence in him, so let the matter rest."

The day following we started early, and before dinner time we reached Sandford. I met sober faces and cold hands on my arrival, but tried to choke down my feelings as best I could, knowing that a lane, though ever so long, must have a turn. I received daily visits from the pastor of our church, who gave me a prayer book and wished me to learn some of the prayers; but I returned the book, saying I wished to be led and taught by one who said, "Take my yoke upon you, and learn of me."

CHAPTER X.

The day was beautiful as ever eyes witnessed, and on the checkered lattice the sun shone gold-like through the green leaves, intermingled with bright purple blossoms; and all was quiet in the household, and all the duties of domestic toil for that day was over. My brother Esick Lyon and his wife had gone to a neighboring town on business, and I was the only occupant of the premises. I had seated myself in a place convenient to notice the the door of the millinery establishment, attending part of my duty at that post also. I was now drawn into a train of meditation, while my needle was my right hand companion; and, although it had an eye, it shed not a tear over my bitter memories of the past, and made not an apology for half-uttered grievances. "Are you alone?" said a voice which I readily recognized as my cousins. "Yes, I am alone; come in, Esther. Why did you not come sooner?" I asked, as she carelessly drew up a chair close to me. "What have you been thinking about? your eyes look red, E. M. What is the matter?" she continued, as she bent over with her elbows on her knees, in a listening attitude. "Dear Esther," at last I said, "you cannot know how it grieves me to think how unwise some have acted toward me; I have been treated as though I was some guilty culprit trying to escape the hand of justice. Shame on the instigator of such mischief; and as to the story that I was obstinate, and would not leave Colesville unless I was forced, that is not true. And now I am watched so close all the time I dare not stir out of the house five minutes before they are looking for me." "I wonder how they dare leave you to-day," said my cousin, laughingly, and continued, " E. M., did you know your uncle was in the grove with a horse and buggy at the time cousin Esick Lyon talked with you?" "I did not know of it; never heard of it until now. O, Esther Nash, you surprise me; and did he intend taking me at that time?" "Yes, he did." "Well, that is why Mr. Sherer held my hand so firmly; I really thought he was crazy. He told me to go with him, and tried to drag me farther and farther down the road. I did not know then that uncle was in the neighborhood, until he rode up to the door at Sarah's; but they were all defeated in that plan. O, Esther, to think of kidnapping a poor little inoffensive girl! Only think of a big man like uncle making such a heroic conquest! He ought to be proud of even the attempt."

Here the talk ended, with a shrug of the shoulders and a hearty laugh. "I must go," said Esther, putting on her sunbonnet. "Don't hurry away so quickly, dear cousin, I shall be lonely." "We expect company to-morrow, and I must help; now look on the bright side," she said, as she tripped off to the hotel, whose proprietor was David Nash, and who probably some of my readers will recognize, as he spent the last of his days in Oshkosh, Wisconsin. But I must hasten with my narrative; and knowing the value of time, I will make the best use possible of that which is allotted to me, knowing that each moment, as it flies, will never return.

After quietude was once more established in our circle, the pastor, as was his custom, came to visit me. This time, however, was something special. He told me there would be a meeting at the church the day following, and he wished me to attend; also, it immediately concerned me, etc. I did not intend to be obstinate, but my feelings revolted against it. I went, however, as the meeting was expressly for the purpose of bringing me to an account.

I was now before the church to say what I could in my own defense; for, until I had made reconciliation to the church I could not be permitted at the communion table. The time came for me to reply to the complaint entered against me, and I arose and told them the charges brought against me were incorrect, and I was very sorry that so much hard labor had been done under false colors; but this I would say, for the satisfaction of the church, that inasmuch as I had been the means of so much dissatisfaction, I felt heartily sorry, and hoped that God and the church would pardon that mistake. This seemed to be all that was necessary, and they gave me the hand of fellowship, and here the trouble ended.

CHAPTER XI.

Now the sun shone out brightly after a storm of strife, and I felt myself at liberty. The culpability of the past had disappeared within the folds of foggy suggestions, and as I hoped, had landed and buried up in the sea of falsehoods, its legitimate mould. I now felt the load was removed, and I was no longer treated as a stranger in a strange land. My aunt, Mrs. Nash, was now, as I noticed, making preliminary arrangements for a ride, as I had heard her giving orders to the hostler to clean the carriage, and reserve the fleet team for her use. The next morning she came in and said she was getting up a party to go to the town of Guilford, and asked my brother's wife if she would be one of the number. "Most assuredly," answered H. "I have been wishing to go on a visit for a number of weeks; in fact, aunt, Deacon Jewel will think, will blame, will disown me, if I don't visit him soon." "O, no; not so bad as that," my aunt said laughingly, "Deacon Jewell is not a man who invents evil." "Aunt, can I go?" "Of course you must. Now girls, be ready early; I will start at seven A. M.; now be ready, the team won't stand a moment." The next morning found us moving rapidly toward Guilford. My aunt was a model for a landlady; she was large and well adapted to her station, which she nobly filled, most elegantly, in every department of her occupation. To see her smile was enough to make one feel welcome and at home. I arrived at my father's house in time for dinner, and once more partook of a repast at my father's

4

table, with my parents and brothers and sisters. I was happy to get home once more. "Home, sweet home!" Did ever words reach a prodigal's ear which sounded more sweet than those to mine? O, what a comfort it is to get home; although we have wandered long from the home of our childhood and the fold of the good shepherd, what peace fills our aching hearts the moment we the welcome voice proclaim — "Rejoice, my house!"

Will you, dear reader, meet your unworthy friend in that home which is prepared by our Redeemer's own hands, where we can see the smiling face of Him whose invitation is to all; and when a few more days of suffering scenes are finished, will you then meet me in our heavenly home? That home, dear readers, is not as far off as many believe it to be; it is here on this earth, and above us, and all around and about us; it is illimitable and spiritual, and can only be discerned by the spirit. They need not the light of the sun nor the moon, for our Heavenly Father giveth them light.

Now I was once more in the fold of my father's house, and in the society of my beloved sister Jane. Braiding straw bonnets was still the unrelenting custom and occupation while at home, although we were accustomed to this work at an early age, besides going to the academy for five years; and now, after serving my time at millinery for two years, I will leave my readers to judge whether my time was spent in idleness. I now resumed my straw work with my sister, and as we did dot attend school at this time, it was work, work, work, with our straw, in the same attitude from morning to night, and not unfrequently until a very late hour, also. This was the everlasting routine of the monotonous life of the straw-braider. However, we enjoyed times of recreation. Our mother was not as exacting as all this, and if we worked early and late it was at our own option, and the result of our own ambition, and as we termed it, "gaining time." We enjoyed our old theatrical performances, the same as when we were younger, and longed to call back the memories of the past, our bright days of childhood.

Seating ourselves one evening beneath a beech tree, to listen to the cheering notes of birds, the sound of the busy crowd had ceased and were joining in with the feathered tribes in musical harmony. The sun, too, had long since sank behind the autumn-tinted trees, and a robin near us sleepily singing its last notes; and the sound of our father's flute and our brother's drum, called us from our resting place and we marched homeward, keeping time with the martial music. The caprice of youth; ah, how fleeting, fleeting! the fairies, the ghosts, the water nymphs, all float before our vision.

"Well, the night-fall closed in upon you," said mother as we skipped into the sitting room. "Yes, we were planning for the future, mother." "Do you think you will have a future mother?" said our mamma. "Yes, and you will have future girls, too, by the appearance of that straw pile. Isn't it splendid?" "O, yes, it looks beautiful, so white and fine." "Is it prepared with the finest gauge?" "No; I will want those bonnets all finished before the gimp, or trimming," said my mother.

> I wonder not that some are straight;
> Nature has her perfections;
> The dwarfed, the twisted also blend
> In all of her collections.

At this period nothing transpired to obstruct our onward prosperity and peace. But the human heart is ever active, and who can say whether it will beat for our happiness or our misery? for the human heart is deceitful above all things.

CHAPTER XII.

Now, with regard to what is termed apparitions, or ghosts — this is a subject we hardly dare to approach, for the very reason that we see no just grounds on which to build our faith. I will, however, relate somewhat of a mystery in my experience, and leave my readers to decide according to their own opinion. I am aware that there are various views concerning those mysteries; yet we all have equal rights to judge of those matters according to each one's tastes, which are generally as various as their countenances.

Once I awoke from a sound sleep; my thoughts were on things relating to what had transpired during my stay at my sister's in Colesville. Why did not my father come or send after me when he heard of my intention to join the Mormon church? Why did they give a power of attorney to disgrace and ignominiously drag away their poor child among those who could not have the feelings of a kind and tender parent? As these thoughts were suggested to my mind, I arose and passed through the room where our servant girl was sleeping, and our parent's room also, and on the porch. My parents were sleeping sweetly, and my opening and closing the doors of each apartment did not disturb the inmates in the least. This was apparent, as the loud breathing could be heard from every sleeping apartment. The moon had climbed its highest summit, and as I was viewing it and the stars, the work of God's hands, and pensively listening to the slow clinking of the distant cow bell, and the steady chippering of the katy-did, suddenly there arose from the ground a personage, about three rods from where I stood on the verandah. This person was dressed in dark, and a dark cloak covered her shoulders. I at once thought it my sister, who probably had undertaken to pass a joke on me, and had thrown herself flat on the ground for this purpose, after which to frighten me by rising up. I therefore commenced talking to her, and called "Jane;" but she gave no answer. She then stepped toward me; I looked at her a few moments, I then stepped toward her. I could now almost reach her; but I found it was no one I had ever seen. She now came so near I could plainly see that her hair was mixed with gray. After we looked at each other for some moments, a chill passed over me, and with a withering shudder I left the apparation and went into the house. I then watched her from the window; she stood in the same attitude for at least a half hour, and then gliding slowly along for about twenty yards, she sank in an instant into the ground; I saw her disappear as plainly as ever I saw anything by bright moonlight.

I then thought of waking my parents to tell them what I had seen, but could not make up my mind to do so. I then looked to see what time it was, and it was light enough to see distinctly. The time was almost two o'clock in the morning. I then went to the servant girl's room and told her the ghost story. She immediately dressed and we went out; I told her the place where she arose, also where she disappeared. We made a considerable noise, and at Clara's suggestion we went into all parts of the premises to find what I knew was not to be found, for I saw the ghost disappear out of sight. This probably was suggestive of good, as I now had something to think of, rather than to doubt the sincerity of the love of my parents. Nothing of any importance transpired, excepting the routine of everyday life, and the common course of business. I confess my feelings were of a peculiar nature at this period; but my religious views were strictly the same as when I could say "My Lord and my God" for the first time. I prayed that my life should be spent in the service of my God, and my example, too, should lead many to Christ. O, how I love that ever blessed name; I love it because there is "no other name given under heaven whereby we can be saved," only through the name of Jesus.

CHAPTER XIII.

A SINGULAR PRESENTIMENT.

In the autumn of the year, when silence prevailed through the household, and also the outward world seemed in slumber, a thought came into my mind that my sister Sarah and her husband, Newell Knight, would come within an hour or two. I tried to abandon the thought, but it still sounded in my mind, over and over again. I could not think of anything else. Finally, I said to mother that my impression was that Sarah and her husband would be there within two hours. This astonished my mother, and she wondered how I could think they would come, as we had not heard from them for several months. I then said I would go to one of the neighbors and wait their coming, for the time would seem tiresome. However, I was soon in the company of the old lady, with whom I loved to visit. But my stay was of short duration, for here came my little brother with his silken locks waving in the wind. "Sarah has come," he said, laughing; "She has come!" I soon proved this assertion, to my own astonishment, as well as to the surprise of all of the household. We met as loving sisters meet. This strange presentiment seemed to baffle our skill to overcome in a degree possible to enter into conversation for a time, as we found it difficult to collect our usual decision of thought.

This was my sister, from whose house I had been once compelled to go on account of their being Mormons; and, strange as it may appear, my sister prevailed on my parents to let me go with them when they returned home; and yet more strange when, as if by some unknown power, I was baptized and confirmed in the Mormon church the next Sabbath after! How it thus happened I will ask my readers to explain, for that intention had not entered my heart when I left my father's house; and I look back with surprise to this day, when I think of those awful days of temptation when I united with the Mormon church. I verily thought I was in the way of my duty, for Christ said, " He that loveth father or mother, brother or sister more than me is not worthy of me."

My sister Sarah was a kind and loving sister; no one could be more kind and no one could be more truthful; so having the utmost confidence in her integrity, it is not strange that I, who was much younger, should coincide with her without any detriment to myself. We are told to " prove all things, and hold fast that which good." This maxim is applicable in this case as well as to mortals. The truth is, women covet knowledge in this as in other things. The pursuit of knowledge, as regards them, is always attended with difficulties. Another fact is, from our birth to our death we are the slaves of prejudice and of circumstances.

The winter following I went with several others to Kirtland, Ohio. They were establishing a Mormon church in that thriving little village. The members now numbered about one hundred persons, the greater part of whom were the brightest and best of the community, merchants, lawyers and doctors. All were united in the belief that God had set his hand again — the second time — to recover the house of Israel. Those people of whom I have just spoken all seemed to feel an interest in the Church of Latter Day Saints (as they styled themselves). I felt as a stranger, and longed to go back to my home; and many a night I spent in weeping for thus leaving my father's house. And I will truthfully say I was not the only one who had thus been led away by those false teachers, for many a house had been deserted and many a family broken up on this account, not only in America, but also in England, Norway, Scotland, Germany, and in Palestine; in fact all parts of the world are partial witnesses to this strange and dangerous delusion.

The Mormon elders were sent out into all parts, to build up churches; Kirtland being the place called by the Saints, one of the stakes of Zion, to prepare to go to the land of promise. Missouri was called the hill of Zion, a land that flows with milk and honey. People were now coming from all parts of the world, and Kirtland was filled with emigrants preparing to go to Missouri. The Colesville church was expected the following summer, and I looked forward to their coming, for I could then enjoy the sweet society of my beloved sister. Preparations were in progress for a final exit to the Hill of Zion; all was hurry and laying plans for the journey; property was sold at auction for half its value. Joseph Smith was the one who dictated in all matters relative to alleviating those who were officially detained in other business. The Colesville church had now arrived, but would necessarily stay until the committee should give directions from Missouri, for them and other churches which were constantly coming into Kirtland, as all things were ordered to be done in order and in wisdom, by Joseph Smith, the prophet.

CHAPTER XIV.

We were detained a few months in Kirtland, and during this time my sister was preparing, as all others were, to be ready whenever the word came to go to Missouri. I remember, as we were busily engaged, I said to her that I had but little faith in Mormonism, and would much rather go home. "How absurd you talk," she said. "Did you not ask God for a witness?"

"Most assuredly, I made this an item in a special manner," I replied. "Well, did you ever get an answer?". "Now sister," I said, "I will tell you all about that. It is probable you will remember soon after you made this request that I should ask God for a witness, I came into the house one day, and looking very pale and frightened, you asked me what made so great a change in my looks; but feeling as I did, I gave no answer. I will now explain all. I have said I went into the woods, and after selecting a place, I knelt in prayer, and as I was earnestly engaged, there came three loud blows on the log, so near me that I felt the wind of the sudden strokes visibly. I then arose, and on looking around I could see nothing. All was still; not even a leaf stirred to break the death-like silence. I then ran to the house, as frightened as when you saw me looking so pale." "Did you take that as evidence of the truth of the Mormons?" asked my sister. "Not by any means," I replied; "I took it exactly the reverse. God's works are in love and tenderness. Indeed, I never could make out what this could mean; sometimes I have thought this was the work of the devil to deceive me, my dear sister." This reminds me of what Christ said: "And when he putteth forth his own sheep, he goeth before them, and the sheep follow him, for they know his voice; and a stranger will they not follow, but will flee from him, for they know not the voice of a stranger."

Now, after the above conversation, Sarah said: "And this is why your faith is lacking, is it?" "The reason," I said, "is simply this: The bible carries with it a spirit of conviction; the book of Mormon is totally void of the spirit of conviction; the bible begets a living faith; the book of Mormon is too mysterious to beget any. Finally, I am not afraid to venture my hopes of happiness on the bible, while I should be afraid to risk my eternal all on the other." I deeply lamented that I had ever been so foolish as to fall in with anything so absurd and unreasonable, the votaries of which I am unable to tell whether they really are to be pitied rather than censured. There were now hundreds who were called people of good sense and judgment, men who were valued in good society; yet they were firm believers in Mormonism. I will say, as regards polygamy, it was not yet thought of or mentioned among the Mormons. I am willing to be qualified to this assertion. I mention this fact because there are those who think it has been practiced in the church from the first. This, however, is a mistake, and we will not lay more to their charge than they are absolutely deserving. The probability is they will not fall short in this respect when they are weighed in the balance.

Now, as time advanced, the little church from Colesville received word from those commissioners who were sent by the church to Missouri to look out lands, and, as preparation had already been made for the journey, we all started for the Ohio river in wagons — twenty-four in number, twelve in each company. The company I was in was called Newell Knight's, and we started one day in advance of the others, as provisions could be more readily purchased for twelve teams than for twenty-four. People all along the road stared at us as they would at a circus or a caravan, and our appearance did not deceive the public eye. We most truly were a band of pilgrims, started out to seek a better country. On arriving at the Ohio river, at a place called Big Beaver, we put up at hotels and awaited the second company's arrival. Fortunately there were no crying children in our band. Our patronage was not partial to only one hotel, and this gave us an opportunity to receive the generous hospitality of all the boarding houses in this little village.

The next day we all embarked on a steamboat bound for Cincinnati; from thence to the Missouri river. In our journey Joseph Smith and Sidney Rigdon came on board the boat; this was not expected when we left Kirtland. However, I noticed there was something which we did not all understand. I did not criticise the matter very closely, as it did not concern me, therefore I will only mention a remark which I accidentally heard made by Sidney Rigdon in conversation with Joseph Smith and the officials of the Colesville church. It was this: "I wish my name was buried in oblivion," at the same time bringing his hand down with violence upon his knee. Another circumstance I will also mention: I observed that Smith and Rigdon were not seen in the day time while they were on the boat. The inference which I drew from these facts was, that they expected officers of the law were in close pursuit of them. However, we accomplished our journey without any molestation. We were told we were the most peaceable and quiet emigrants they had ever carried west; "no profanity, no bad language, no gambling and no drinking," said the captain, as he was good-naturedly talking with some of the head ones of our company. We were nearing the place of our landing.

We now resorted to flat boats to take us up the river to the mouth of Big Blue, in Jackson county, and to the ferry landing, and here we disembarked and our journey was ended, except a few miles by land into the country. My first impression was, "is this the Hill of Zion, a land prepared for the Saints?" And as I had been informed of the direction, I walked on in advance of the company, not intending to lose sight of those who were shortly coming. I walked on slowly, thinking how strange it was to think of this being the Hill of Zion, when suddenly an Indian made his appearance, with a rifle on his shoulder. This was the first Indian I had ever seen, and I must confess I was considerably startled at his appearance. When he saw me he took a roundabout way, and did not look at me as I noticed. I had seen one of the so-called Lamonites, and also the so-called land of promise.

CHAPTER XV.

The church had become numerous within a year or two after we arrived, and we were in a new country, without farming machinery to work with, the effects of which aroused them to something still more difficult than to purchase farms; therefore teams were dispatched to St. Louis for the purpose of obtaining the necessary implements for farming purposes. This required the space of four days to accomplish, in making one trip. The demand for farming tools increased, as the Mormons were constantly coming into Jackson county. Consequently teams were constantly on the road to St. Louis, not only for farming machinery, but for other necessaries, such as mercantile goods, all of such as were needful, both in groceries and dry goods. Probably it is indispensably requisite to say that all the money belonging to the wealthy members of the Mormon community was put into the church treasury; and one man had the entire charge of all financial affairs. Had it not been thus, there would have been great suffering among the poor and the aged, who were in this way both fed and clothed Probably this is the origin of the report that they had all things in common; and this is true. The poor were provided for, as well as those who had put their money into the treasury. They were all satisfied and happy to all appearance, and all seemed to enjoy themselves.

The time to break prairie had come, and it was a strange sight indeed, to see four or five yoke of oxen turning up the rich soil. Fencing and other improvements went on in rapid succession. Cabins were built and prepared for families as fast as time, money and labor could accomplish the work; and our homes in this new country presented a prosperous appearance — almost equal to Paradise itself — and our peace and happiness, as we flattered ourselves, were not in a great degree deficient to that of our first parents in the garden of Eden, as no labor or painstaking was spared in the cultivation of flowers and shrubbery of a choice selection, from a green-house in St. Louis market. I was not of a criticising nature, consequently I had not as yet seen anything to stagger my faith in the sincerity of the Saints. I can furthermore say, I was pleased with the country, and became more and more reconciled trying daily, in my own mind, to make the differences appear consistent.

In the year 1833 I was married to a young man from our own neighborhood, in the state of New York — a nephew of the governor of the state of Vermont. He was of rich parentage, and of high respectability; and having received the many honors and hospitalities and congratulations of our numerous friends, and spending a few weeks in traveling, we located on a farm in a settlement near my sister Sarah's pleasant home. It was at this period we promised ourselves a happy, enjoyable life; a life of peace and plenty; a life devoted to the service of God; a life of benevolence to those who were unfortunate and needy; a life to bind up the broken-hearted and comfort the mourner; a life to teach by example, as well as precept; a life of charity; a life to show to the world that we had been with Christ, and learned of Him.

On several occasions we received intelligence that the inhabitants of Jackson county were displeased at the idea of so many coming into the county. They said the range for their cattle would be taken by the Mormon cattle, and the "shuck" was devoured by the Mormon pigs; and they boldly declared they would not suffer this so to be; and to maintain their integrity, complaint was made to the state authorities and the governor issued a command that every Mormon should leave the county at once. But the Saints refused to obey the order. The Mormons said they had paid their money just the same as others. "Yes, we have paid for our land," said they, "and in accordance with the laws of the land and the constitution, we have, therefore, the same right as other citizens, and we propose to stick to our farms." On hearing this, the Missourians rose *en masse* and demanded all fire-arms, and I believe they succeeded in getting a few old shot guns and old axes belonging to the Mormons, and then rode off, with their broad-rimmed hats and blanket overcoats, which costume was in those days characteristic of a fully developed Missourian. Deeming their courage without a rival, they twirled their broad-rimmed hats in the triumphant thought that they had disarmed the Mormons. They visited us the next Sabbath in order to ascertain our intention as regarded the governor's command. The Saints replied that they would resist unto blood. Then war commenced between the two parties; the former declaring if we were not gone by the Sabbath following they would exterminate every man, woman and child remaining; and when they visited us again they would visit us with terror. Among those who was thus breathing out threats, a man by the name of Mr. E. Campbell was sent out to their horses, which were standing before the door, to get a loaded pistol. The horse pistol was brought into the house and preparations were made for that which had been previously threatened; and stepping up to my sister-in-law with his murderous weapon, he said: "Madam, where is your husband? tell me the truth; do you see this weapon, which is only waiting for your heart's blood?" My sister-in-law calmly replied that she knew nothing as to his whereabouts, and could not tell anything more about it. "Well, can you tell us when the Yankee's intend to leave this county?" said he. "No, I cannot," she replied. "Now, madam," said the leader, "if you are not gone by next Sunday (stamping his foot, which caused the house to tremble), do you now understand? I say death will be your portion if you are here over another Sunday." So saying, they all mounted their horses and hastened away to another Mormon settlement, where they dealt out the same horrible abuse.

The day following we received intelligence that the Missourians were close upon us; and no sooner had the news reached our settlement than every man flew to their arms, drew them from their hiding places, loaded, shouldered and started to the scene of action. A battle ensued, and many were killed and several wounded, both of the Saints and Missourians. This difficulty lasted several months, and the Mormons, not willing to give up their farms, suffered great damages and endured many very great hardships, being deprived of the privilege of lodging in their own houses at night; and there was no safety in burning lights or speaking a loud word after nightfall. This order of things was kept up until late in autumn. During this time the governor's command was repeated, that the Saints should leave Jackson county, and that Clay county should be a place of safety for them. Colonel Atchison was, to all appearance, a friend of the Mormon church, and through his counsel and advice the Saints agreed on the conditions that, if Jackson county people would buy their improvements and farms with the produce, then, for the sake of peace, they would leave the county. The counsel of Colonel Atchison was, that the Mormons would act more wisely to move directly, as cold weather would set in before they could possibly get arrangements made comfortable for their families. "In view of this, I will see that you all have your rights," said the Colonel. "You come and get your produce, and your farms can be sold at your own time; but get your families in comfortable quarters and then look after your property, is my advice," he said. His advice was not very pleasing to the Latter Day Saints. However, if there was a "must" in the case, there remained no alternative, and we gathered up what little we could take in wagons and crossed the Missouri river and pitched our tents in Clay county, on the bank of the river. Many were taken with chills and fever, and altogether the Mormons presented a pitiable spectacle.

At this distressing period, every man who was able to work went to the farmers for employment, in order to maintain their families. I will say for the praise of Clay county that a more free and generous people I never saw in any country. The Colesville church, together with twenty or thirty other branches of the Mormon church, had already arrived at this point, and more were on the way, and many were camped on the river below, and some above us. We lived in tents until winter set in, and did our cooking out in the wind and storms. Log heaps were our parlor stoves, and the cold, wet ground our velvet carpets, and the crying of little children our piano forte; while the shivering, sick people hovered over the burning log piles here and there, some begging for cold water and others for hot coffee or tea. We found it convenient to have near neighbors; if we wished to borrow we had not far to go after it; and the hottest log heap was hunted out by those whose chill was just coming on. The snow covered our sleeping tents, and the scene reminded one of the gathering of the house of Israel. Every tent was covered with snow six or eight inches deep. It now looked more like a city than before the snow fall. In our tent my husband had obtained boards and made a floor, and then, spreading the large buffalo robe over the boards, made our sleeping tent look comfortable, and our pride was to keep it tidy.

In the latter part of winter the Mormons built cabins, and made them convenient and comfortable also. The floors were made of puncheons and the roofing made of oak shingles, which served wondrously well in the place of a better material. As people, although we did not enjoy the legal rights of civilized citizens, yet we maintained the right of freedom of conscience; neither could we be deprived of the liberty of serving God according to our views. We also had the liberty of thought, and according to the constitution the liberty of speech also. Joseph Smith and Sidney Rigdon had long since left Missouri and gone to Kirtland, where the Saints were gathering, and where the former was president of the Kirtland banking house, and Sidney Rigdon vice-president; therefore, their attention and interest were unmistakably requisite. Not only this, but the fact that the Mormon church was building a temple; this also called them to that place to oversee the work.

CHAPTER XVI.

Now a new joy sprang up in our cottage home. A little daughter had come to brighten our hopes, to cheer and strengthen our efforts along life's rugged pathway. Then came beautiful spring, with its birds and flowers, and the river running not far from our little cottage door. All was quietude and harmony; no railing, threatening mob to disturb us then, for we had the promise of a peaceful and safe possession. Here let me pause for one moment and ask one question: Dear reader, how would you enjoy this? Think you, the notes of birds, or the beautiful tinted flowers, or the flowing river, would soothe your aching, injured heart and spirit; driven from your hard earned homes, and compelled to wander without home or shelter; being buffetted and smitten, until the blood ran down the clothes of those who tried to obtain their grain and other produce in Jackson county; after being bruised with sled stakes, they were brought home by those of the company who were fortunate enough to escape their blood-stained hands. This was done without provocation. I beg leave to say that my faith in Mormonism never was firmly established, by any means, and I never could see the consistency of this mysterious faith; but give me the true gospel of Christ, and then I feel that my feet are firmly fixed upon the rock; and without hesitation I will say, I am a believer in consistency in every case. That which is right is under all circumstances approvable. Nevertheless, two wrongs did not make one right in this case. How true it is, that the wicked pass on from one degree of wickedness to another; they pass on and are punished. If the Mormons were a deceived people, there were many well meaning people among them who had toiled to procure homes for themselves, and it was not according to the law of God or man to drive them from their possessions. "I allow," said my husband, one day as we were talking this matter over, "that there is a time when 'forbearance ceases to be a virtue;' and in my opinion in this example the blame unmistakably rests upon our persecutors. It is right to a certain extent to show charity and pity to those who err, and more especially to those who are innocent, and still misled by others." "That is true," I said, "and I am glad to hear you make that remark." "May I ask you why you are glad?" said my husband. "Well, that looks to me as though you considered the Mormons a misled people." "Very well, supposing they are a deluded sect, is that any reason why a greater calamity should come upon us? Is it not better to pity than chide the erring? This is not the way to reclaim the wicked. 'Weep with those who weep, and rejoice with those who rejoice.'"

And let me say, furthermore, if a being upon whom the allwise Creator has bestowed the finer feelings of a sympathetic nature, smothers and buries within the deep recesses of its own heart all those feelings which awaken at the misfortune of others, is it doing wrong by disobeying the laws which a Supreme Being has established, who would hide his face to blush and weep over a withered and broken flower? it is so life like; or some frail bud, which we have especially nourished long and tenderly, that has prematurely and suddenly withered away like the last soft tint of the declining sun upon a summer sky, nature is all beautiful; and, were it not intended that our hearts should be stirred even each emotion therein, by the sight of so much purity, why, then these beauties which surround us? What mission have the flowers but to teach us our own fraility, and inspire us to good and generous actions. And thus, if we would look into objects which the breath of the Almighty has brought into existence, we would draw therefrom some very useful and needed lessons.

"Life," says an able writer, "is like the flow of a mighty river that is ever hastening onward to the goal that is beyond, until it is almost lost in immensity; and yet still preserving its identity; and we shall preserve our own individuality while wandering through the illimited space, and our life and character formed here, will correspond with that life which shall be hereafter." Then why not strive to beautify the soul while here, and throw around it every charm that could allure an angel from its bright abode? The human soul is like a bright bird that flutters and flings itself against the bars of its dark prison house, striving in vain to free itself and soar away to some more congenial clime, where the weary, throbbing heart shall be still and the sweet gentle voice of its dear mate would soothe it to rest. The little bird that blithly hops from tree to tree, strives not to stifle the feelings that are swelling in its little breast, but pours them forth in one long, thrilling gush of melody; filling the air with its cry of joy, or its shrill-piercing notes of woe, until its song seems to die away and is lost, perhaps in some distant realm of the spirit-land where they are caught up and re-echoed by the glorious Paradisiacal hosts, until its silvery chime fills all the arches of yonder glorious heaven.

What a charming thought, that we are attended by some pure being from the celestial world, and that our departed friends are ever waiting to administer to our happiness; to whisper words of comfort, of love and wisdom, and point us onward to that haven of rest! Since life can do but little save to allure us for a while, with its soft balmy air or the fragrance of flowers and the melody of birds and the flow of pure streamlets, let us look upward to the throne of light, and entreat the good, the beautiful and the true, to come and dwell with us; and by their pure and loving influence, allure our minds to dwell on things heavenly, and assist us to cultivate our heart's emotions aright, that we may ever "rejoice with those who rejoice, and weep with those who weep."

CHAPTER XVII.

We are still living in our cabins. Our church, or rather the building in which we worshipped, was built very large and commodious, suitable to accommodate eight families; and on the Sabbath and one evening in every week the church assembled for worship in the building. There were two large fire-places, the chimneys of which were built of sticks and mortar; built very particular and straight. The logs of this building were hewed, and the entire building elegantly whitewashed outwardly, and papered inside; all of which was very creditably done. It was, in fact, a parsonage, as no other than the elders of the church lived in that building. It was called the White House, from the fact that there was no other cabin whitewashed, except this, in our settlement. Some of our Gentile neighbors would attend meeting on the Sabbath, probably through curiosity, as it is my opinion they never entered a place of worship in all their life before. The voice of prayer and singing averted their attention from the hunting ground of the dense forest, and they seemed to enjoy sitting with us in meeting.

> "The sound of a church-going bell
> These valleys and rocks never heard;
> Never sighed at the sound of a knell,
> Or smiled when the Sabbath appeared."

"The proud willows seem to waive over our humble cottage," said my husband, as we were enjoying the cool evening breeze from the river; "and their proud tops whisper defiance to our rising above our present condition," he continued, "yet my darling, we are young, and our means to procure another home is not by any means exhausted, so you need not weep over our misfortune. Our little Nellie will be provided for, God being my helper. Another thing I have to comfort me, that is there is not a spot upon God's throne that will appear against me in any respect, which has brought this calamity upon us, I have wronged no one, and if you remember, my dear, he continued, they told us if we would renounce Mormonism, we could remain there and be respectable citizens among them." "Yes," I replied hesitatingly, "I remember one Sabbath as they met us as we were going home from church." "Yes, that is the time; and about the respectability, what did you think of that," asked my husband, laughingly. "I was just going to say the mantle would fall upon us in that respect."

We found it not in our nature to settle down in poverty and degradation, and resolved to put forth our best energies to acquire a better position. However, it was not the order of the Mormon church for any of the members to separate from the main body, and the Colesville church remained together. Therefore our experience in many respects differed from that of other branches of the church.

Some of the Jackson county persecutors visited our side of the river, in companies of four and five in number; what their mission was we did not learn; however, in one instance they came with a flat boat, and after drawing the boat upon the land, they shouldered their rifles and went over the bluffs in pursuit of game.

While they tarried, some of the Mormons finding the boat, took off a plank and bored several places in the bottom of the boat and placed the plank back as before. The men came, and finding the boat all right, as they supposed, started over, and before they reached the middle of the river the boat sank, and two of the men were drowned. One of the men who were drowned was Mr. E. Campbell, the one who threatened extermination to our men, women and children in Jackson county. The other unfortunate man was one of Campbell's own accomplices.

The time had now arrived to commence farming, and we rented a farm two miles from the river. This farm was ample for two or three families. According to this consideration, my husband and two of his brothers, also his mother and sister, Mrs. Rogers, removed to this more convenient place for each family. We now enjoyed a peaceable habitation; although our Gentile neighbors were slaveholders, yet they were warm-hearted, friendly and obliging. The second year we were afflicted with chills and fever, which continued through the entire season, and not one escaped this dreadful malady. There were none on whom we could depend for even a drink of water. I have visited hospitals, but never witnessed any sickness as distressing as this. Newell Knight, my brother-in-law, lived among the bluffs, a mile and a half from the river. A thick forest surrounded their wigwam; for it was truly an Indian camp, or wigwam. I think I never saw a more broken piece of land, the bluffs running up to a point, the top of which was so sharp it would be impossible for a man to stand with both feet on the summit. Away down amidst those massive mountains my sister and her infant child are sleeping in one casket. They are folded together in that mansion where the lambs of Christ are gathered; there is Sarah and her infant.

>Count me thy sister, O, thou weary one,
>   Struggling along amid the toils of life;
>Standing erect, though almost overcome,
>   Waging a warfare in unequal strife.
>
>Count me thy sister, O, thou sore oppressed,
>   Wearing a bond which fetters thee to earth;
>Enduring wrongs which ne'er can be redress'd,
>   'Till death shall issue in thy heavenly birth.
>
>Count me thy sister, tried and tempted soul,
>   Seeking for light, though smothered by the dark;
>Lured by the siren's voice, yet keeping whole
>   The soul's purest virtue and the spotless heart.

> Count me thy sister, O, thou son of Him,
>   Who with patient tenderness loveth all;
> Help me to do thy will, forsake all sin,
>   That I may hear thy sweet voice shortly call,
>   And own me thine, thy sister — we shall meet.

After sister Sarah's departure I sent my parents the sad intelligence of our loss. The answer was undelayed, and they uniformly partook with me in our bereavement; not as those who have no hope, for we were not separated forever; only a few short days and we will meet again in a more congenial clime, where sorrow and death will not disturb our peace.

The chills and fever continued with us. It seemed to have an attraction which was hard to shake off. I took my sister's sick child, a little boy two years old, and now I had two sick babies, besides being sick myself with chills and fever, and also a paralytic stroke came upon me, from rinsing clothes in cold water. My husband was also ill until winter, and in fact until after the holidays. This gigantic disease we found more difficult to contend with than it was for Israel to contend with the Canaanites; and as we began to recover, the demand for food would have tempted us to become parasitical in order to obtain a good rich meal of victuals. In fact, so exhorbitant was our demand that a quarter of beef, in the eyes of those three families, looked like a small pittance.

The winter was a severe one, and as a matter of course we endured very many hardships, and in those terrible chastisements we were remembered in mercy; and although in a country of wicked practices, in some measure, yet forbearance on our part was a harbinger of safety, and prudence our maxim. At all events we were blessed with a better retreat than horse-racing, gambling, drinking and profanity, even to a Mormon meeting on the Sabbath, where prayer was wont to be made, and where the voice of singing made the forest ring with melody, and rejoice at a sound it never had heard.

A year had now passed since my sister's death. Newell Knight had been to Kirtland, and returning with a wife they took little Samuel to their own home. Having now been freed from the care of this interesting little boy, another precious treasure filled our hearts with joy. It was another beautiful little girl. had come to cheer us, amid the toil and care of our pilgrim life, and enrich our ideas of the usefulness of our existence, and the importance of a well refined example. The church now assembled to make arrangements for purchasing farms. It was therefore put to vote in this assembly, and carried, that Newell Knight, I. Morly, and J. Carrel, were elected to go to Caldwell county, Missouri, and look out lands for the Mormon church. On returning, they brought a good report, that the site was far superior to any they had previously seen; a good grazing country, plenty of timber and good water, and few inhabitants. We at once began to pull up stakes again for another removal; and the time was well occupied until we were again settled, in our new homes. The church soon built up a city on a rolling, expansive prairie. One could feel at home, and be satisfied with the prospect. My husband bought farming land and timber sufficient for a lifetime; he also built a dwelling house in the city. Our city lot was one acre of ground, and all required buildings were properly erected. Finding this part of the country far superior to Jackson county, the Saints proposed to abide there permanently. Preparations were being made for building a temple upon the most sightly place in the city of Far West, for this was the name; but this could not be done until the ground was dedicated, and the corner stone must be also dedicated, or some ceremony performed, and the prophet Joseph Smith was the only efficient one who had the power or authority to officiate in such matters.

In the year 1835 (as near as my memory serves me), in the latter part of June, the bishop of the church sent for Brother Joseph, as he was called, to come to Far West city immediately, on important business. At this period the bank of Kirtland was under good operation. However, Joseph made due arrangements in consideration of the banking business, and came to Far West, accompanied by Sidney Rigdon. They remained in Far West until after the fourth of July. Preparations were made for the dedication, and nothing remained excepting to roll the stone to its proper place; and this was to be accomplished on the day of the fourth of July. Independence day came; the Saints assembled at the bower. The speaker ascended to the stand accompanied by Smith. The speaker, which was no other than Rigdon, and his attendant, took their seats and awaited the assemblage. Our city was visited on this occasion by people from a distance, among whom were some of the broad-rims, as was noticed by the Saints. The speaker and attendant came down from the stand and proceeded to the place where the corner stone of the temple was to be laid. Joseph Smith made a prayer, after which the Saints sung a piece composed for this purpose. Then a few remarks were made by L. Pattrage, the bishop of the church, and one of the high priests, and Parley Pratt, an elder of the church; then singing, and the benediction, pronounced by Joseph Smith. After which they proceeded to their respective seats. The constitution was read by P. P. Pratt. Sidney Rigdon followed by delivering an address on the liberty and freedom of the American people, and wound up by saying he defied the people of Caldwell county to drive us from Far West and the country adjoining; that the Great Jehovah would interfere and fight our battles for us. This was confirmed by the Saints, and three loud and long cheers and amens rent the air. At this a very great excitement arose among the old settlers, and Rigdon's life could not have been insured for five coppers. The people were all crazy with excitement, running and rushing to and from, and tumbling one over another in every direction. I must say I was rejoiced to make exit with my two little children, with the help of my husband.

This remark from Mr. Rigdon was productive of much evil. We endured threatening on every hand. Troops were sent to Far West to keep down insurrection. Our gardens and barns were plundered. The church tried in vain to secure their property, but found that nothing was safe from the hands of the militia. At this point I observed a secret Mormon meeting was called, and my conclusion was that they were forming a treaty. However, this was not the case. Their plan was to form a club called "Danites." Those were of the rough class of people; those who, through good fortune, rather than good management, escaped from the law of justice and found protection in the Mormon church. Of what the ceremony of initiating members consisted, I am not able to say, as this was a profound secret. This club formed their own laws and customs, and each officer and member was apprised of each one's success or defeat. The mission of Danites is to rob, murder and steal, or do any wicked act, especially to those who leave the church. Nothing is considered too hostile for one who leaves the Mormon church. "Better not to have known the way, than after they have known it to depart from it." This is their maxim, and a general principle throughout the church; and this principle is just as unalterable as the laws of the Medes and Persians — among the Mormons.

At this period three hundred mounted men were stationed among us, and their aim was to take the town and hold us prisoners until we were set at liberty, by each family separating out and moving off by themselves, as soon as prepa-ations could be made. Two of those militia officers boarded with us while we remained in Far West. Some time previous to this state of affairs I had begged of my husband to leave the Mormons; to sell what property we could for ready money, and leave the remainder, for we would be obliged to leave all we had if we remained there. This was now clearly apparent to my husband, and to our desponding hearts. After being apprised of the depredations of the Danites in the surrounding country, we became more and more averse to the hazardous management of the so-called Latter Day Saints, and 1 for one strove hard to free myself from this awful state of things; and, under the consideration that I could speak out my views about the inconsistency of Mormonism (having the officers placed in our reach), I felt safe to say as I thought about this matter, and not feel that I would be given over to the mercy of the Danites, who were at this time lurking in ambush far out in the country, and at night they came forth in pursuit of spoil, coming into Far West just before the break of day.

CHAPTER XVIII.

"Have you seen the spoil which was brought into town?" This question came from a young lady who came to our well for water, a little before sunrise one fine morning. "No, I have not," I answered. "Well, make some errand over, and as you pass that" (pointing to a wagon), "just, for pity sake, cast your eye into the wagon and see the plunder; then come into the house and Mrs. Stebbins will give you something to take home, for we know not who is watching." According to Miss Correll's suggestion, I put on my sunbonnet and went over; I passed several steps beyond the wagon, and then turned back to the wagon. I looked in, and there was dead geese and chickens, and a pig dressed without scalding; an old plow, two or three shovels, three or four hoes, and grain in sacks, and corn and firewood. I then passed into the house, where we enjoyed a hearty laugh. Mrs. Stebbins gave me something done up in a paper to take home, in order to keep down suspicion, if any were criticising our movements. When I opened the paper her sunbonnet dropped out.

Many days and nights we labored to accomplish what we most desired, even to the sacrifice of all we possessed. And, in conclusive views of our aim we departed from the state of Missouri, leaving all we possessed, except our team and a few household goods. Having three little ones now to care for, and not sufficient means to make another beginning, my husband became disheartened; his courage in some degree faltered. Yet this he tried to conceal from me. I saw all; would that my knowledge of this could become a night dream, from which I could wake and say, "It's a dream."

Our purpose for a stopping place was decided upon after leaving Far West. Our company consisted of my husband's two brothers, his mother and sister; we had three covered wagons in the company. Pittsfield, Illinois, was agreed upon for our present locality. After arriving there we were guests at Springer's hotel for some weeks, or until a proper location for farming could be procured. Winter being over, my husband and his eldest brother, who was also a farmer, had taken land of Colonel

Ross and Captain Davis, of Pittsfield; and now it remained with us to test the truth of the proverb which says: "Better is a dry morsel and quietness therewith, than a house full of sacrifices, with strife;" although the alarming condition of my husband's health often brought my courage low, as to even a dry morsel. The consumption, which was his disease, laid a sure foundation for my fears. The farm which we occupied was one-half mile from Pittsfield, and was not by any means productive. However, Colonel Ross was not a selfish man; I believe he gave us nearly all we raised the first year, and the second year we left the place and removed to Pittsfield before the crops were gathered, as we found it difficult in the latter part of the season to get water. Another consideration was, we were away from any school, church or neighbors. There was yet another: In the village I could work at the millinery business, and thus help my husband a little. Our children now numbered four, and my husband's youngest brother remained with us. We appreciated the privilege of living in a land of peace, and felt at times that we had nothing to trouble us; no hostile foe to encounter; no threatening mob to dread when we retired at night; even the recollection of which fills me with astonishment. That we were bravehearted enough to sojourn in such a land of wickedness and strife, and endure such hardships as we endured, and for such a long period, is surprising.

My husband's eldest brother, his sister and mother, all moved to Nauvoo, where the Mormons had gathered after leaving Far West. This desolate place was called Commerce, at this period, and there were not more than a dozen inhabitants there. It was afterwards called Nauvoo, by the Mormons, a Hebrew name, the interpretation of which is, "Pleasant Land." The Mormons all gathered at this point, and improvements were rapidly made. Every improvement was calculated to give place for others of the Mormon society to come to; so that all things should, so far as possible, be prepared before hand for those who were coming from Kirtland.

We often received news from our relatives in Nauvoo relative to the proceedings and purposes of the church; and, through newspapers, we observed many reports which were published, probably by mistaken individuals, and so far as we knew of these by experience, we gave no heed to them. However, in many respects the analogy of these reports were not detected only by those who had the experience. This calls my attention to one thing in particular: One beautiful morning my husband came in with a newspaper in his hand, saying he had something he wished to read to me. It was the testimony of an English girl against Brigham Young and others. She stated that while on a visit from her school to Nauvoo, to her mother's, she called on a lady friend, and while conversing, her friend invited her to go with her to her husband's store. Miss Brotherton accepted the invitation, and they walked on together, Miss B. observing by the way, her friend's cordiality and unusual politeness. On arriving at Mr. K's store, they were politely seated by a good-natured clerk; Mr. K. also appeared very courteous, which was indeed agreeable, after which he waited upon his wife. Turning to the teacher, he said: "Would you not like a dress of some of those choice pieces of goods, Miss Brotherton?" "Not to-day," said she, "I am not prepared to do trading." "Here are very choice poplins," he replied, " would any of those suit your taste?" "Not to-day, sir," said Miss B. But look," he continued, "you shall have a present of one of those handsome poplins, if you like." "O, no," was her answer, and at the same time she blushingly proposed to wait until she should draw her school money; "then I will call and get what I think is necessary," she added. "You had better get a dress to-day," said Mrs. K., coaxingly. "You are foolish if you do not, as you now have time to make it during vacation." "That is most truly the case," was the response; "but, dear woman, the weather is too warm to work upon such goods;" at the same time taking her dainty little handkerchief to dry her forehead. "The heat is intense," said Mrs. K. "Suppose we go up into the parlor and rest awhile, it is cool and pleasant up there; besides, we can enjoy a social chat together, and get rested and refreshed." Martha complied with this kind offer and ascended the stairs with Mrs. K. Upon reaching the landing above, Mrs. K. took a key from her pocket and unlocked the door. The key which she used was a large, old-fashioned one, such as they used in old times to unlock large, heavy doors with; then pushing the door open bade Martha enter. She stepped hurriedly in and saw at a glance the room was large and beautifully furnished. As her attention was at once drawn to the east end of the room, she thought that was not the room where Mrs. K. intended to stop, but further on, probably; and on looking around she discovered that

Mrs. K. had not yet entered the apartment. In the east end she saw Joseph Smith, Hiram Smith, Mr. Taylor, Brigham Young, and several others whom she did not know. They were all seated, and seemingly enjoying themselves amazingly well. She went to the door and found it fastened. Brigham, finding her embarrassed, stepped up to her, bringing with him a chair, and told her to sit down, that Mrs. K. would return soon. She thereupon composed herself as best she could, in hopes that Mrs. K. would come and explain all. So, after talking with Mr. Young a few moments, Brigham drew his chair close to her and put his arm around her waist, in spite of her efforts to defend herself. She therefore thought to use artifice. Mr. Young began: "Have you heard of the new order of things which has been revealed to the prophet?" "I have not heard of any in particular," said Martha, "although I am aware that brother Joseph often receives revelations; however, I have not the opportunity which some are favored with, as I am engaged in my school in the country most of my time; and if there is anything new I would like so much to hear it." "Very true," said Brigham; "and now if I should propose marriage to you would you accept it?" Martha studied for an answer, and then said: "You have a wife, have you not?" "O, yes; but if the Lord should give a revelation to that effect, would you accept me?" "If I was sure it came from God I should most assuredly accept it." "This order came by a revelation from God," replied Brigham, "through his prophet Joseph; and if you will give your permission we will be united." "Well," said Martha, "this is something new to me, indeed; I never heard of this order until now, and, if my mother will give her consent, I will agreeably adhere to your strange proposal." "How soon can you see your mother?" asked Brigham, seeming to be in haste to bring about the welcome day. "O, I can see her and talk this matter over within an hour," she replied. "Indeed, I never take steps without I first consult mother. I will acquaint her of the fact that it is a revelation from God, and I am satisfied she will agree to it." Saying this she started to go. Brigham also arose, and taking a night key from his vest pocket he unlocked the door; Brigham saying, as he took out a splendid gold watch, "You will return within one hour — half past ten — you will call again at half past eleven, sure?" "Yes," said Martha, smartly, as she pinned her lace shawl more closely.

Within ten minutes she reached her mother's house. As she entered, her mother observed something strange in her daughter's appearance, and began to interrogate the matter. As Mrs. Brotherton began to question her, Martha raised both hands, exclaiming: "O, mother, mother! let the dinner and everything go to-day, and put on your bonnet and shawl and go with me over the river, and while you are getting ready I will tell you in a few words what has happened. Do hurry! Where is brother? Call him to row the boat. Are you ready? do hurry, dear mother." " Martha, my child," said the mother, " what has happened?" "Well, brother Joseph has given a revelation that men can have as many wives as they can support, and Brigham wants to marry me; the time is half gone; put down the window curtains and lock the door. Your basket, yes; now run, and when we are in the middle of the river we are out of all danger. Now, brother, stretch those little arms of yours, and paddle for dear life; perhaps we can get out of their reach before they know of our leaving." " Yes," said her brother, " if we are not observed by Danites in our haste to get away from Nauvoo; these islands are infested with them at this time." "Well, never mind, please do hurry," said the sister. "Do not hurry me, I am tired out now, and I am not very stout," he replied. "Well, let me." So saying, Martha took the paddle and almost lifted the boat from the water. Within a few moments they were out of danger; the paddle dropped from her swollen, delicate hands, and she fainted and fell to the bottom of the boat. Her mother now remembered a vial of ammonia in her basket; this, with the help of water which her brother administered, was sufficient to bring life again to her exhausted and frightened nerves. On looking to their whereabouts they found they had floated two or three miles down the river, and the rocky bluffs on the landing shore prevented them from stepping on land for a mile or two below; so they could but pass on slowly and calmly, laying plans for the future. They finally came to a little village and there stayed two or three days or a week perhaps, before Martha went to Carthage, the county seat of Hancock county, where she was qualified to this statement, and probably never visited Nauvoo again.

After reading the above, my husband folded the paper, making a few remarks in doubtful accents on what he had read, and we both agreed that it was too absurd to believe, as we never had heard anything of the kind before. It did not look reasonable that people who professed christianity would so far listen to the evil one as to carry out such base principles.

Something of more importance now awakened my most sensitive powers — more important to me at least; for, although of the story just related I was doubtful, of one thing I was not in the least doubt. Our little flock numbered five. My husband was passing away. Each rising sun proclaimed that his stay would not be long with us; the dreadful disease had laid claim to its victim. He lingered some time, and then sank into the tomb, fully prepared for the Master's use.

> Dearest husband, thou hast left us,
>   Here thy loss we deeply feel;
> But 'tis God who hath bereft us,
>   He can all our sorrows heal.
>
> Peaceful be thy silent slumber;
>   Peaceful be thy grave so low,
> Thou no more will join our number,
>   Thou no more our sorrows know.
>
> Yet again we hope to meet thee
>   When the dreams of life are fled,
> There, in heaven, we hope to greet thee,
>   Where no farewell tear is shed.

He sleeps in the cemetery in Pittsfield, Illinois.

How dark the shadows gathered around me, seeming to dash all courage and hope far beyond my reach; and despondency and grief are those besetments which baffle every effort to rise above the present forebodings of that which then appeared unavoidable — want. My pretended friends soon came in possession of what my husband left for me and his little children; and now nothing remained except myself and five little fatherless babes, the eldest nine years and the youngest six months old. Those I intended to keep with me, at all events; they were all I had left, and I determined to keep my little flock with me; and I often flattered myself that as they grew to be larger, their companionship would be a great blessing and comfort to me. I was advised to move to Nauvoo, where my husband's relatives could assist me. The weather was at this period very warm and sultry; however, I ventured the journey, which was one hundred miles; and besides, I had with me a sick babe. My child's illness was of a serious nature, requiring all my attention.

This period of my life will last on memory's pages while life remains, and then I shall leave it for those who survive me to read, when my spirit shall have passed away to a happier clime, where sickness, sorrow and death cannot enter.

CHAPTER XIX.

Just as my infant was so dangerously ill that it could not be left a moment, news came to me by one of my neighbors that all four of my children were floating down the river in a skiff; that they were about in the middle of the stream, where the water ran swift. I immediately took my sick child, throwing the blanket over it, and ran to the river bank. I saw the skiff, but the distance was so far I could not see the little sailors. The skiff looked very small; I watched the boat for some time, and at last I saw two men pulling toward them with all speed. Lucky for them that no steamboat was passing at that time to upset their little craft in the waves which always follow.

At this period I had been in Nauvoo about three months, as near as I can remember, and owing to the illness of my child I could not pay much attention to the other little ones, and they were feeling at full liberty to go where and when they pleased. The family who resided in the same house with me were strangers, and I said but little to them. The lady was a native of the East Indies and her husband was an English gentleman and a Mormon elder. They were very pleasant, and I believe tried to live christians. Taking the liberty to inquire their name they told me it was Brotherton. I made no reply, but like Mary of old, pondered those things in my heart. "Can it be," thought I, "that this man is a relative of Martha Brotherton?" However, I kept all to myself. Some weeks after we were all seated in the front room; the evening was made beautiful by the brightness of the moon, which had risen to its summit, and cast its silvery light upon the still waters of the great Mississippi. This room where we sat was radiant with the reflection of the moon upon the water; and not a word was spoken to disturb our thoughts for some time. At last I broke the silence, and said: "Mr. Brotherton, are you willing that I should ask you a question?" He replied that I could ask any question I saw proper, and if it was anything he could answer he would most willingly do so. "Yes," said Mrs. B., "if there is anythine you wish which we can do, we are perfectly willing. It appears you are not without trouble as well as ourselves and many others; you need not doubt our sincerity," she continued, "but say what you like and it shall go no farther." "The question is this," I replied, "are you a relative of Miss Martha Brotherton, who published a piece in a Carthage paper against Brigham Young?" "Yes, I am her brother," was the response. "Well, do you know her to be a truthful girl?" I said; "please pardon my inquisitiveness." "Most assuredly, yes," said her brother. "She published nothing but the truth." "One more question and I am done," I said. "Do you know that polygamy is practiced in the church?" "I do," he answered firmly; "but we must not mention this to any one." "I shall not stay here," I replied. "As soon as my child is well enough I shall leave this horrible wicked place."

This explains all; no good Christian mothers; no one to say one word of sympathy or consolation; no mutual sensibility; no Good Samaritan to administer relief to the needs of the sick and suffering; this was all plain to me now; there was no light in their sin-darkened hearts; no love of God, and it was no wonder they knew nothing of me or my distress. These were the thoughts which were passing in my mind, when Mrs. B. remarked in a low voice, "We are intending to go away as soon as possible; but we keep all this to ourselves, and we advise you to do the same; if we wish safety we must be wise." "Exactly so," I said, in a low voice, "I know something of this by experience." "All right," said Mrs. B. After the above conversation we retired. I could not believe that all the good had turned to bitterness, and there remained not one who was laboring for God and heaven. O for a display of God's providence; for something more genuine, more congenial and high, noble; more pure, more peaceful, more strengthening, more glorious! I thought upon these things with a sorrowing heart; and, as I studied upon them, those words came to me as if spoken by some good spirit: "He that putteth his trust in Me shall never be ashamed." This was a pleasing thought, that there was one in whom we could trust and never be ashamed; and the conclusion of the whole matter is, to "fear God and keep His commandments, for this is the whole duty of man; for God will bring every work into judgment, with every secret thing, whether it be good or whether it be evil."

I could make no confidant of any one; and in consideration of my own safety I kept my mind to myself. My own helplessness, as well as that of many others, was a defense to those whose barbarous principles were to take the advantage of our weakness in making known their unlawful deeds. This we dare not undertake, as our lives were dear to us. The Danites were close upon the track of those who otherwise would have strangled polygamy in its infancy.

Having now found relief for my invalid child, whose illness had been such a burden for both child and mother, for the period of a year, and as I began gradually to find my attention a little more relieved as he grew stronger, I now felt the unmistakable need of putting my very best energies into practice; therefore, after investigating the probability of my being competent to teach a small school, I drew up a paper and proceeded to get signers for an elementary school. I found no difficulty in getting twenty scholars within the space of two hours time. I agreed to teach sixty days, at two dollars a scholar. Previous to this I had sold my team for a house and lot in town, in the expectation of selling the property when I removed east, as I had for some time contemplated; but having no deed as yet, I found myself unable to make any change in this direction, and this is why I remained in Nauvoo up to this period. It was now getting into autumn. I had left my last cow in Pittsfield, and I now had an opportunity offered of having her driven up to Nauvoo for me; but the man returned without the cow, and told me that those having charge of her refused to let her go, and so kept her for their trouble. My belief is, that the man who offered to drive her for me, or the man who had had charge of her, sold the cow and put the money in his own pocket. I know not who it was, but there is an ever watchful eye who knows and sees the one who robbed the widow and fatherless children. I mention such events only to show the evil which lurks in the dark recesses of the human heart, and whosoever is guilty of such things will find when too late that the interest of such petty thieving will be gathered in and compounded.

My school was progressing, and as it was kept in my own house, it was considered a blessing both by myself and little ones, that we were not compelled to trudge off through snow or rain to a cold school house. Some of my patrons paid in advance. My firewood was provided ready for use at my door, and all seemed highly pleased with the way the school was conducted. While teaching this school, a note was sent to me desiring my attendance at a wedding at Deacon Lovey's. I at once began to question who it could be. There was no one in Deacon Lovey's family who was old enough to marry, thought I. Probably it is some one who dares not belong to the family. However, I attended at the hour appointed, and when the parties advanced it was Deacon Lovey himself, leading an old maid by the name of Elmyra Mack. I was more astonished now than I ever was. There sat his other wife, looking perfectly happy. The ceremony was said, after which a lively time ensued, and all seemed joyous and full af merriment. But for my own part I was dumb; and when the question was asked me how I enjoyed the evening, I made reply that I had talked so much in school I felt very tired; I therefore prayed to be excused, and left the merry party to their own hilarity. I thought this matter over, and resolved on leaving Nauvoo as speedily as possible, making my arrangements to that effect. I, as yet, had not obtained my deed; also two of my little girls had for some time past been living with their father's relatives in the country. Those two facts were obstacles which remained to be settled by a plural number, and I felt at a loss to know how it would turn out. I had not as yet made known my intentions, and patiently awaited the close of my school and the return of spring. I closed school the first of April. Then my garden was plowed and a portion of it planted. The spring was pleasant and warm; the sun shone out brightly, and the birds with their sweet notes welcomed the queen of the season.

I now visited the man with whom my business was intrusted, and told him I had come to see about my deed, or something to show that I had paid for the house and lot. He declined giving any security, but said he would make that all right. Mrs. Smith invited me to stay to dinner, but I refused, saying I had obligated myself to return in two hours. While I stopped a few moments in conversation with Mrs. Smith, her husband rode up in a splendid carriage and asked if I would not ride, as he was going on business the way I was to return. I accepted the offer, and on our way he asked if I had tried to inform myself of the great work which was enjoined upon us as God's children? I told him I knew of nothing but to serve God with an honest and upright heart. "This is not all," he said; "God's work is progressive, ever onward; as his children grow more numerous their wants increase, doing for us all we wish or desire; if we trust in Him, He has promised us all things, if we live faithful to him. And now, since these promises are left us for our benefit, why not accept?" "Accept what?"

I asked. "Accept and obey God's command," he replied, "which He has given through His servant Joseph; that is, a man can have all the wives he can get if he marries them for time and eternity; that is, if he takes care of them in time they will also be his in eternity; for the glory of man is the woman; the more women he has the more glory will crown him in heaven. And now, if when you consider this properly, and think it better to have one who will provide for and protect you, let me know your mind, and all will be well." Here we parted, and I was left to think over the conversation which had passed. He little thought of what passed my mind while he conversed with me on the way. Ah, little did he imagine that which almost came from my lips, and would have formed into words had it not been at the peril of my life. "A wise head keeps a close mouth." "Death and life are in the power of the tongue, and they that love it shall eat the fruit thereof."—Prov., 18: 21.

The next morning was a beautiful one, one upon whose brightness the happy spirits love to come down to earth and sweeten every cup of sorrow by imparting to their sweetness and purity, in the melody of birds or the bursting forth of some unexpected flower. What more could mortals ask, while thus welcomed to earth and heaven by a new born day like this? Peace of mind, in the great giver of all good; my conscience also bearing me witness that I am His and He is mine.

I rented my place to Deacon Lovey and received part of the rent for four years' possession, not revealing my intentions to my nearest neighbors, and dreaded the approach of my aforesaid assailant. This man of whom I have spoken once belonged to the Presbyterian church, and was an influential member. He possessed sobriety, and to all outward appearance was an honest man. He was very neat in his attire, and his general deportment was excellent — well fitted to gain the good will and high esteem of all with whom he associated. I mention these facts, as there are those who are misinformed as regards the Mormons, in many respects; but believing, also knowing, that their sins in their pretended religious views, are exhorbitant. I find it not in my heart to make any allowance for their unchristian-like, and also their unloyal deed. At the time of which I am writing, I felt in my heart that which my tongue dare not utter.

I left Nauvoo for a period of four years, then to return for my two little girls, in hopes that kind providence would mete out changes for our most earnest wishes, in this our helpless condition. My feelings, I must acknowledge, was not parallel with the circumstances by which I was governed in respect to leaving my two little girls in Nauvoo among the Mormons. However, our relatives in that place were not polygamists; yet they were firm believers in the first principles of the Mormon belief. I kept my plans to myself as much as possible, and started on my journey before any one knew of my intentions; or at least but few were informed of the fact. Had I made known my plans publicly, I probably never should have made my escape from that place. I arrived at my friends in Ohio with three little children. After spending the usual time in visiting my friends, I rented a house and again established a home, with my little family. I was rejoiced to find myself among people who feared God and regarded the law of our country, and could rest in safety and security from those with whom there was no safety.

CHAPTER XX.

My aim in writing this history is to give an account of the commencement of the Mormon church. It is not taken from hearsay, or any history, but is a true statement of the facts concerning the origin of the Mormon belief. I therefore ask pardon for writing so much of my own experience, but this train of consequences forbids its exclusion.

Finding my efforts a little dashed when I tried the millinery business, I soon found it useless to try to make a fortune, and came to the decision to only make a good living, and be content with food and raiment. Those little ones who remained far away, among a people in whom there remained no veracity, I often talked of. They were in my mind constantly, ever remaining as a shadow over a running brook, while the dashing waters of the cares of this life hurried onward. Those shadows seemed to vibrate continually in my memory. Yet there is a time for all things, and I awaited the time to advance and bring about the welcome day when those little ones should be gathered to my own care and protection.

One year and six months had now passed since my arrival in Ohio. I had repeatedly received letters from Nauvoo, one of which brought tidings of the sad death of Newell Knight, who was sent as one of the commissioners to Salt Lake in pursuit of a land of safety for the Latter Day Saints. This was at an early period, and no travel had broken the way except that of gold miners to California. Those commissioners traveled as far as the Rocky Mountains, and here they were compelled to yield to their merciless doom — starvation. I received intelligence also of many arrests in Nauvoo, and also imprisonments, and many courts were called. In this case the Mormons always affirmed innocence in behalf of a Mormon. This state of things was carried on ever after the Danites were organized. I will now give the detail of a letter which I received from my sister-in-law, from Nauvoo, reading as follows:

"NAUVOO, Ill., May 14, 1838.

"DEAR SISTER: I will spare no time in addressing you, as I have dreadful news to write. The church was awe-stricken yesterday by the sad news that brother Joseph Smith and Hiram were both shot in Carthage jail; Hiram was shot on the floor, and brother Joseph was shot while trying to make his escape through the window. Sixteen bullets passed through his body, and he fell from the window on the outside of the jail, which was twenty feet. They had their trial in court and were put back to await another trial, and a mob gathered around the jail, forty in number, and forced an entrance, killing three and wounding several others; all of which was perpetrated within ten minutes time. Some one of the mob saw Smith's body on the outside and stabbed him through and through with his sword, saying as he did so, 'You are the man that killed my father.' Our doors are draped with crape, and the church is dressed in deep mourning.

ANN CLEAVELAND."

This was astonishing news to me, and I have tried in many ways to find out where they were buried; but this is not known to any except those who laid them away. I have been told the church thought they would be raised from the dead, and kept them several days in expectation of seeing that miracle performed; but they began to putrify to such a degree they were obliged to put them away. How true this is I am not prepared to assert; and yet my authority is such that I can feel safe to vindicate the assertion as truth, knowing as I do that such absurdities have prevailed from the commencement of the church. I therefore do not feel at liberty to discard this saying as untrue. The Danites are kept in constant knowledge of all secrets of the Mormon society, and while I remained with the church after those secret clubs were formed, I felt in almost constant alarm. I now and then noticed groups of Danites away off in some retired place, busily talking, and they looked like anything but good men. Their appearance more resembled fiends, as near as I could judge; and many is the time I have wondered to myself how I should make my escape from among them.

I was about changing my situation to fill a vacancy as nurse; I therefore found places for my children, and expected within two or three weeks to be released, and again return to my former home with my family. The gentleman who employed me was Mr. Joshua Foabs, of Wayne, Ashtabula county, Ohio. One morning in March I started to go and see my little boy, who was staying with a lady some four miles distant. Mr. Foabs offered me a horse to ride, and also told me of a nearer way than the general public road. I therefore confidently rode on until I came to a saw mill. The water was dashing over the embankment so furiously

I was fearful that the animal would get frightened at its roaring, so I led the horse across on the ice. My feet had no more than reached the land when the ice suddenly gave way and went dashing over the embankment. I succeeded in saving the horse, as he happened to be very nimble, and keeping the reins fast in my hands I led the animal to a saw log and sat down until I was a little more composed. The horse, too, trembled piteously.

When I returned, Mr. Foabs told me he had just noticed a paragraph in his paper announcing the expected and immediate exodus of the Mormon church to Utah territory; also asking me if I had any children in Nauvoo. I told him I had two little girls remaining there. "Do you wish to get them?" he asked. "Most assuredly, I must have them," I answered; "of course I must have my children," I said. "Well, if that is the case I will see what can be done for you," he replied. The next day he tried at two or three places for money to help get my children, but to no purpose. He stated the fact to me, but said I need not fear, he would let me have the money, but thought probably some others would be glad to help. "But you shall go," he continued; "I will do all myself." Tears filled my eyes, and I turned to Mrs. Foabs to hide my emotions from her husband. Mrs. Foabs was on the sofa, and when I looked at her she smiled pleasantly and approvingly at what her husband had just told me. I never can forget that angel countenance. Mrs. Foabs had lost her voice, yet she could hear, but could not speak above a whisper.

I started with a family who were moving to Burlington, Iowa, by the name of Allen, a near neighbor of Mr. Foabs, who were company for me all the way to Nauvoo. I landed there the second day of May, at 2 o'clock A. M. It was raining, and dark as Egypt. The mud was black and sticky, and it was one mile to the nearest house. I noticed on leaving the boat a young lady who had landed, for the light shone brightly on the wharf. I asked her if she was acquainted in Nauvoo. The answer was, "No." She then said she had come to see her brother before he went to Salt Lake. The boat was now leaving the wharf, and we had found the road which led to the temple, and then we were in total darkness, rain and mud. However, we managed to keep the road, as the weeds soon reminded us when we were out of the way; so long as we were in the mud we considered ourselves all right. If I had not had my trunk to carry we could have helped ourselves much better. We were obliged to sit down every now and then, and it served for a seat to rest ourselves. "Have you ever heard of the Danites?" I asked my companion. "No, what are they?" she asked. "Well, they are a set of men who are appointed by the leaders of the Mormon church to arrest any who are leaving the church and bring them back here." I paused, for I heard two persons hurriedly passing us. "What is that?" she whispered, tremblingly. "I do not know," was the answer. "Do you think they were Danites?" "No," I said, perceiving she was intimidated. "O, no; they are some persons who came from the wharf, probably;" yet I had my own opinion about it, but kept this to myself. We hurried as fast as the darkness would permit. The rain had made our clothes very wet and heavy; the mud also had collected on our boots until it seemed that it was impossible to make much headway; besides, I had my trunk to carry. We cleaned off our boots on the weeds and sat down to rest. I could just perceive the shape of the rise of ground where the temple stood; and, further observation presented a light, although very dim. I told my companion I saw a light, but she could not see it. We again took the trunk and traveled on for some time. "Yes,

I see the light now," said the patient girl. I thought her patience endured bravely; but she said she had much rather help me than to try to find the way alone. But now we had got almost to the house where the light was. "What if they are Danites?" said the girl. "O, well, if they are they will know we have just come to Nauvoo, and they in all probability won't ask any questions; but here is the house." I rapped at the door, and after a considerable bustle in the house, a woman unlocked it and let us in. "Can we find a shelter here until daylight?" I inquired. The woman hesitated and then said: "If you can put up with poor fare." "All we ask is a place to stop until it is light enough to find our friends," we said, "so make yourself no trouble." She parted her bed and made us a bed on the floor; and now we had a place to rest our weary limbs for at least two hours. We told her we came from the boat and the night was dark and rainy; that we were very thankful to get a place to stay as comfortable as that was. She then told us they were getting ready to move, and everything was so unsettled and comfortless, she said she would be rejoiced when they were on the road. "Ah, you are going east?" I said. "No, we are going to Salt Lake. See," she said, pointing to a wagon wheel in the corner of the room, "we have to take one wheel off of our wagon and bring it into the house to keep the mob from running the wagon off in the night."

The chickens now proclaiming the approach of day, made my heart leap for joy. The thought that I should soon see my little girls caused feelings which none but a mother's heart can know. Daylight had once more dawned upon us; and we were on our way to the temple. Here we separated, and each one went in search of her friends. After procuring a conveyance, I soon arrived at the place desired. My arrival was very unexpected, and one of my little girls did not know me, as she was only four years old when I left Nauvoo, and the other eight years old. My sorrowful heart could not find utterance, when I saw my neglected, fatherless children — neglected because their aunt and grandmother were too busily engaged to attend to anything except to make tents and other necessaries for their journey to Salt Lake, and then they intended to get the children ready also. I could not talk. I therefore spent a few days looking to see the changes that had taken place since I left; my two little girls holding my hands and joyfully hopping along by my side. "Mother," said Elizabeth, "are you going back to Ohio? I want to go with you if you are; Ed. and Angeline don't treat me very well, and Ansro makes me black his boots, and if I don't he whips me. Do you think that's right, mamma?" "No, my child, he is old enough to be a gentleman now, but his ideas of gentility are not as they should be. But never mind, this will all be right," I replied.

CHAPTER XXI.

I often looked upon those children with fond hopes of taking them with me; but when the time came that I should be interrogated on this point, then probably it would be soon enough to make known my purpose. I did not feel flattered when I so often heard them called handsome, for I could see how they looked as well as others; I could see that nature had formed them with many charms, so far as features, form and complexion were concerned; and I felt a determination that those two little girls should not be raised in the Mormon belief if it should be necessary to put the law in force.

I could readily get help in this direction, as the Mormons had but few friends in the county.

Sarah lived with her aunt and grandmother, while the other lived with her uncle and aunt. Elizabeth was the oldest, being at the age of ten, and Sarah six years old; and I found in those little girls delectableness in their confidence, as I could unfold my mind to them without the least fear of exposure. I therefore made plain to them that I had come on purpose after them, and should not return without them. I furthermore told them not to show by their actions that they thought of going with me. While conversing with my sister-in-law one day, she asked if I intended taking the girls with me. I told her I should try and get a deed of my house and lot in the first place, and then we would talk about that. "You can't have Elizabeth; if you think of that, you will be disappointed; I expect to keep her until some one takes her from me, when she is old enough to marry," she said. "Very well," I answered, "then you will take her to Salt Lake?" "Of course I will," was the reply; "she is better off with us than she could be with you; and Ann says she shall keep Sarah." Here the talk ended, for a time. The next day I went to see Mrs. Smith about my deed, and Elizabeth accompanied me, for I did not feel safe to leave them both there, fearing they would send them off, or conceal them from me. I now had an opportunity of telling Elizabeth what I should do if they tried to keep them from me. If nothing else would do, I should get help in Carthage; but I thought it not best to use harshness as long as anything else would answer the purpose. I was now at Mrs. Smith's. She informed me that her business was in court; but if I could wait until June court, she would give me a deed, as she would then have permission from court to give deeds. The matter seemed at a long pause to wait until the June court; however, having some things needful to attend to before I could return, I went about it as speedily as circumstances would allow. I had sewing for my children to do, and had to attend to the sale of my furniture, which I had left in Nauvoo when going to Ohio. This was difficult, as so many had left, and others were about to leave. I therefore employed a good honest man (although a Mormon), to see to the immediate disposition of my furniture, the avails of a small portion of which would be required to clothe my children. The furniture was taken over the river to Mt. Rose, and left for sale.

My daughter Elizabeth lived with her aunt

Roxania, who was the daughter of Elder Rogers, a Methodist minister then residing in the town of Bainbridge, Chenango county, N. Y. It is needful to mention these facts, in order to more fully explain my story; also for other purposes which it is not needful to mention. One day, as I was in conversation with Benjamin and Roxania, I asked them why they did not go to see their father in Bainbridge before going to Salt Lake. Said I, "the road will be left open for you to go when you please to Salt Lake; another thing, your health is not sufficient to endure the hardships of so new a country again as that is at the present time; but when the roads are better traveled, and when they begin to have things in a more comfortable manner, you can then have that enjoyment which, if you should go now, you would be totally deprived of. Now, what do you think about my suggestion?" Benjamin turned around with his back toward me (which always meant approval), and after a few moments he said: "Probably it would be better for us." "We would not need Elizabeth," said his wife, "if we go east; probably you will take her with you?" as she turned to me for the answer. "O, of course I shall take her if you do not need her; that is all right." The night previous to this conversation some one knew of a poor widow who spent the long, weary night in prayer to Him who said He would be the widow's God and guide, and a father to the fatherless. He also said, "If any lack wisdom, let him ask of God, who giveth to all men liberty and upbraideth not." That same widow had made this a subject of prayer for a number of weeks, and this is the work of God, and not hers. "The eyes of the Lord are upon the righteous, and his ears are open unto their cry. The righteous cry and the Lord heareth and delivereth them out of their troubles. Many are the afflictions of the righteous; but the Lord delivereth him out of them all."— Psalms, 24: 15, 17, 19. Only a day or two before this, Roxania told me in plain English that I should not have Elizabeth. This was also written on her countenance. Howbeit, it was written on my heart with something indelible, which never could be erased, "I will have my little girls." I afterwards talked with Ann Cleaveland in regard to taking Sarah Frances with me, and she said it remained for her mother to say concerning that. It was decided that it would be better not to separate the little girls. Thus was it all settled, joyfully settled in my behalf. Yet if I had been two weeks later they would have been gone far beyond my reach. But now a dark cloud gathered, and what this strange foreboding could mean I was at a great loss to understand. Had my friends prevaricated in this way to throw me off my guard, and thus evade, and slip my children away privately? This I could not believe of my good old mother-in-law; she would not stoop so low as that, neither would any of her family. Yet they were very zealous in the Mormon belief, but not in polygamy. I inquired why they did not believe in this also; their answer was that the church had become corrupt, and for an illustration, compared it to a fruit tree — the roots were good and healthy, but the enemy had crept in and was destroying and making nests and webs in some of the branches. This was done through neglect. They have not acted wisely, and for this reason the enemy has obtained a strong hold in many instances; and until these offences are eradicated from the church, they never will prosper. "I am heartily glad to hear that you are not believers in polygamy," said I; "would to God that you were not Mormons." Here the conversation ended.

The next day my husband's youngest brother came in. "I think your faith in Mormonism is very small, or you would not go back among the Gentiles," he said. "You know, George," I replied, "I have three children there." "Very well," said he, "but your children won't save your soul." "Neither will Mormonism save me," I replied. "O, yes; you are an apostate; I thought so, and now have your own words for it." "Well," I responded, "I shall be miserable without my children." "Then," he said, "you prefer your children to the only true and reliable light?" "Not so, George," was my answer; "however, I think a mother is not necessarily compelled to be separated from her children in order to enjoy the true light. Why, George, how unreasonable you talk. Do you know what the unerring way is? I think it is to love God with all the heart, might, mind and strength, and love our neighbor as ourselves; and in order to do this we must be cleansed from all sin, through the blood of Christ." "Ah, but," said George, "we must live up to the requirements, too." "Yes; what have I refused to do which he required?" I asked. "You refuse to go to Salt Lake, which is a command of God," said he. "Yes, but the church was also commanded to go to Missouri, and that was the land of promise; but now He has altered His mind and says Salt Lake is the land of promise," I said. I had gone as far as was prudent, and something called me away in the midst of this conversation.

About the first of July, as near as I remember, my sister-in-law started for the plains with her mother, an old lady over seventy years old, and three little boys. Mr. Cleaveland, her husband, was one who was wounded in a battle in the Mormon war, in Missouri, from which he never recovered, his right arm and right lung almost disabling him for any kind of labor. In this helpless condition, with the weather extremely warm, they bid farewell to their last home in the States, and their friends, to sojourn in a strange land. My feelings, on seeing them depart, were indescribable. My little girls spent the day in weeping, neither tasting food until the next day noon. Brother Benjamin and family also left their home to sojourn among friends in the East. Now we were lonely and disconsolate; none remained on the farm except George and his wife and one child, myself and two children. Some time in June I received my deed, and now, having only a garment or two to finish up, and then nothing remained except going to town after my money, and I should also start for Ohio.

We had heard of considerable sickness in the country adjoining, but had not a distant thought that it would reach us. The next day George and his wife and child were all taken down with this fearful malady. The weather continued oppressively warm and dry; I think I never witnessed so warm a summer since my remembrance. The fever was now gaining ground, and nothing was heard of but distress in the whole country around. Myself and children were also taken ill with this fever, which was considered beyond the skill of any physician to arrest. We were now helpless; no one to assist us until my sister-in-law's mother, Mrs. Commins, was sent for. I am unable to state how long my fever continued before I found relief, as I was delirious most of the time; however, it could not have been more than two or three days. My children's illness turned to the ague, so that part of the time they could help Mrs. Commins. I had taken medicine which had helped me, and feeling anxious to recover, I put forth my best energies to start on my journey. My greatest dread was of being buried in Nauvoo; I had much rather my resting place should be in the bottom of the Mississippi river. I engaged a lady to take me to Nauvoo in her covered carriage, where I could get my furniture money. The covered carriage I thought would protect me from the hot sun. I then charged her to drive slow, as I was too weak to endure the trip, with all the care that could possibly be taken. On arriving there the man had gone over to Mt. Rose and would not return until about sundown. His wife advised me to stay over night, which invitation I accepted, and as I had already gone beyond my strength, I retired to bed, up stairs. There were no blinds to the windows, and the hot sun had sent in its heat during the day, and I fancied a hot bed in a hot house would be far more enjoyable for a sleeping room than this empty, comfortless apartment. This was Saturday, late in the afternoon, probably four or five o'clock. From this hour until ten the next day I saw no human face. Seventeen hours without even a drink of water. Just after I retired I awoke, and could wring the sweat from my my hair and clothes. I expected the lady would come up to see me before bed time, but she did not. It was now very dark, and the sound of distant thunder proclaimed a shower not very far off. When it came it was most terriffic. One peal of thunder after another, in quick succession. It seemed that the horizon was in a complete blaze of liquid fire. The wind and torrents of rain which would terrify a strong person, now filled me with horror; and a sickness which I had not hitherto experienced came over me. I never shall forget that night. The house was so constructed there was no passing from the rooms below up into my room, except from the outside of the building, and the severity of the storm prevented an exit either way. I would gladly have changed places with Lazarus, but could more properly claim the place of the rich man. Howbeit, I survived that dreadful night, and thankful was I to see the dawn of another day; and, in the gray twilight I arose from that horrible couch, and as I passed into the front room I saw a tall figure approaching me, with its ashy and ghostly visage, with long hair in dark masses, hanging in wild confusion over the shoulders. I shrank and staggered back; and in order to show me how I appeared, this ghost shrank and staggered, precisely as one can mock another. On taking the second thought I discovered how feeble my imaginations, how perfectly prostrated my physical strength had become; my appearance, too, was as one just from the tomb. At ten o'clock the lady of the house made her appearance. She came, she said, to know if I wished any breakfast. I told her I would like a cup of tea. She soon returned with the tea and a bit of hard rye bread and a little beef soup. The soup tasted like brine, and the tea tasted like warm water turned out of an old rusty tea pot. The breakfast did not relish, and I knew it was my taste. This lady was very pleasing in all her movements, courteous and obliging, and with all very handsome. She assisted me in putting on my clothes and helped me down the long stairs into her apartment. Her husband gave me the money for which the furniture was sold, and after paying him for his trouble I began to think about going back to my brother-in-laws. Thankful was I to feel so well after such a night of distress. I now thought I should be able to start on my journey in a few days. Those people were Mormons, and were intending to start for Salt Lake as soon as the warm weather subsided. They were remarkably good to me in offering to take me home on a bed in the wagon, and a little girl to hold an an umbrella over me; but now it was nearly noon, and I felt the fever was coming on. They advised me to get to my friends as soon as possible, which just suited me; and as soon as it was possible we were on the way. The reason I did not press the matter was because I heard them say the team had had a hard trip the day previous, so I awaited this kind offer. But now I was not able to make any calculations about anything; the fever was at the highest, and my mind was not capable of care.

The man drove up to the door and called George to come and take me into the house, but George was on the bed very sick; however, Mrs. Cummins and Elizabeth came and helped me into the house and to a bed. Three days later I found myself better, with a will which nothing but death could baffle, and making the best of everything which obstructed my progress. I immediately bent my steps to my determination, and agreeable to this I took my cane — not such as gentlemen use, but one made of a corn stalk — not wholly to support my dignity, either, but to bear up my remarkably weak and feeble frame until it should please my Heavenly Father to place us, forsooth, safely on a boat eastward bound. I engaged a team to take me to my own house in town, then I would be nearer the steamboat landing; for my desire was to start on my journey the very next day. We arrived at the long deserted house, but what could we do here? We had taken particular pains to put up a salt sack of flour and a little cup of salt, in case of emergency; but we had nothing to cook and nothing to cook in. Fortunately I had a bed and trunk, but we had no place to rest ourselves except on the trunk and bed, which was not boxed up, only tied up in a sheet. This answered very well such a time as this, when the whole town was in confusion and so many sick. It would be beyond the art of an able writer to describe the distressing scenes which were daily taking place in Nauvoo at this period.

Night was coming on, and now what should we do for supper? My children had both had the ague that day, and were very sick for a time; but now they were up again. Finally, we talked about what we should do for supper again, and concluded to go without; but we had no dinner and not much breakfast. "Ma, I know where we can get a pan to bake bread in," said Elizabeth. "Is it an iron pan?" I asked. "Yes, but its dreadful rusty," she said, "I'll go and get it." The pan was pulled up out of the grass, and after a good time digging and scraping at the old pan, my girls made a fire out in the door-yard, after building a little stone arch to sit the pan on, according as I told them. This was splendid. In the mean time I had stirred up pancakes with salt and water, and heating the pan and rubbing thoroughly with salt and a bit of brown paper, I managed to bake the cakes without greasing the pan. Those cakes and a cup of cold water made out our repast. We had not finished the cakes when we were surprised to hear the sound of distant thunder. "O, what shall we do?" said the little girls, both speaking at once. Just at this instant I was thinking I should not stay in the old deserted place over night; I could not, for there was no knowing who harbored in the house. Probably every night Danites met there to hold council. Imaginations of this character filled me with horror, knowing that at this period Nauvoo was a poor place for safety. Every movement of the Mormon church indicated rebellion against the civil law and against those whom they termed Gentiles. This term indicates Paganism, applied to those who are skeptical in the Mormon belief. They make no distinction whatever, and the Gentile law is the same to them as the heathen law or customs would be to us. This, however, is a secret belief among them, and a recent feature in the Mormon church; I mean not until they were driven out of Missouri did I ever hear anything of this character advocated among them. However, they stick to the text without variableness or shadow of turning, and the thought that a man of this order should so far elude the commonwealth as to gain a hearing at the seat of government under the American flag, looks strange to all who have had any experience in the Mormon church. Let me here say I would just as soon be called a Parricide as to bear the name of a Mormon, a name which I have always been ashamed of; and yet I can say of a truth that no disgrace is attached to my experience among this people. But I have wandered far from my situation in the deserted house.

The west wind now began to blow furiously, and whatever there remained to be done must be executed speedily, else we would be left in the dark and rain. Elizabeth ran to the nearest neighbor and asked if we could stay there over night. An affirmative answer soon brought her back, accompanied by a boy to take my goods over, also. We had just got our beds arranged, and were all comfortably in bed when the rain descended and the floods came. This was a new brick house, not finished off; up stairs a window was left out, and the chamber floor consisted of loose boards near enough together to step on. My bed happened to be in the right place to catch the rain from the window. The lady of the house, I discovered, had got out of bed and was trying to fasten something up to the window up stairs. There was no man about the premises to assist; the lady tried in vain to secure the window as the storm beat vehemently upon her unprotected form, and she was compelled to yield. Not a word could be heard; the roar of rain and wind was terrible. In the meantime Elizabeth and Sarah had gone to seek a better position. I had crawled up on a dry goods box and wrapped up in wet bed clothes, in order to protect myself from the wind. On looking for my children to beckon them to me, a flash of lightning revealed the place of their retreat, and the water was dripping from their faces and hair. The storm passed gradually away, and as soon as I could be heard, I called my little girls to me and wrapped them up as best I could in wet clothes, and we spent the night in this awful condition. Morning came, and we immediately hailed the glorious welcome dawn to prepare to leave the city of trouble. The sun rose in magnificent splendor, and in the consideration of our night of cruel exposure, we arranged our affairs wondrously well through the day. I got permission to do my washing at the next nearest neighbors, and after putting our bed out to dry, we immediately changed our place and got our breakfast at Mr. Farnsworth's, glad to get where we could get something to eat. We partook of the repast with a relish which we had not hitherto enjoyed for some time. Mrs. Farnsworth assisted in getting the wash water ready for us, and while she thus assisted I, with the help of my cane, walked over to Mr. Fielding's to engage him with his team to take us to the landing, the next morning at 9 o'clock. After resting a few moments, I inquired if Mr. Fielding was at home. His wife said he was fixing his wagon in the back yard, and he would be in presently. I waited a few moments, and while I sat waiting, Mrs. Fielding's baby began to worry, and she gave the child to a boy who came in, saying: "Jim, take Charley out to papa;" and a minute after another ludy came from another room; she also had a child in her arms. She sat down and her child began to cry, and its mother gave it to a little girl and said, "Take Georgy out to his papa." Those two wives of Mr. Fielding's were large, portly, good-looking women; but O, my God! to think of those people being criminals, fit subjects for the penitentiary. I was glad, and even rejoiced to leave that house, and under any other circumstances I should not have spoken to such people or took notice of them, if I had my right mind.

I kept silent on this question; as I had enough to attend to of my own affairs; and another essential thing was, if I had told my mind there remained not one doubt but a fatal result would have occurred, and that speeeily. I returned to my wash room, and with the assistance of my little girls we got along wonderfully well. A doctor visited at Farnsworth's during the day and said I was a plucky woman, for he never saw a person at work as ill as I was. Said he, "You will pay dear for this; and ten chances to one if you ever recover. Your place is in bed; you have a settled, malignant fever, and ought rather to be under the careful treatment of a skillful physician and nurse, than to be so presumptuous." His talk did not affect me though in the least, and we worked on until about sundown. We then hung out the few pieces which had caused us so much hard labor; and while hanging out our little washing I improved the opportunity of telling Elizabeth what we must do; that Mr. Farnsworth had asked me to become his wife, and —. "Well, well; what did you say to him?" "I told him I had no time to attend to such things now, but when I felt more settled, after I got to Salt Lake, I would then think more about such duties, probably." "Now what must we do?" she asked. "Well, we must keep awake to-night, my child; can you, think?" "Yes," said

Elizabeth, "I can keep awake, but it will make you worse." I am sure we did not sleep a wink last night; and such a night! "O, mother, you are killing yourself," said Elizabeth. "Well, my child, if I can get away with you and Sarah Frances, I cannot ask for anything more; if I find I am not going to live, I will place you in the care of some good people on the boat and tell them where to send you, and all about it; but we can keep awake one more night."

After this conversation we had some change to make in our clothing, and as directed by Mrs. Farnsworth, we retired to a small room, probably seven by ten in size. While there, we noticed there was no window except a pane of glass, and that looked out into a wagon shop. It was now getting dark, yet it was as light as early twilight. Just before we were ready to leave the room, my daughter hurriedly exclaimed, "I am afraid this room is not safe for us," pointing to a bloody place on the wall, and a great blood puddle on the floor; and on looking farther, a rifle in one corner, and directly under my feet a trap door. We lost no time in hurrying out, and shuddered as we went. We were now confident there was cause enough to fear that all was not right, as the doctor went out the same direction of this room before mentioned. I cannot say what the doctor's business was, but I have my own opinion about it. Those bloody places looked almost fresh, only dried over a little. The murder was committed, probably the previous night during that storm. "Only a little longer," was sounded and repeated in my mind; "only a little longer, and all will be well." This was the assurance, and this was what gave me strength and fortitude. If I had offered any remarks in opposition to their belief, I should have shared the same fate of many others. We were startled several times during the night, but found ourselves all safe at last, when morning came. That day we rejoiced to think we should bid adieu to the City of Destruction, and after eating a hurried breakfast we set about getting ourselves ready to depart; and we were happy, although we resembled patients just free from a long occupancy of infirmary lodgings.

At 9 o'clock A. M. the team for which we had been in long waiting stood before the door, and after settling with my host, we started for the landing. On arriving there we unexpectedly found a house of entertainment at the wharf; and on making inquiry, I found that a boat going eastward was not expected until the next day. I concluded to let patience have its perfect work, and in view of this I set my mind at rest. That day my children shook harder with the ague than ever before, and at 3 o'clock P. M. my fever returned double fold, and we were shown to a bed up stairs. I do not recollect having any attention, and only remember that we were all on one bed up stairs. This is all I can recollect, until about 12 o'clock that night. I was then awakened by the sound of some one coming up stairs with heavy boots, and I shuddered from head to foot. I now thought my time had come. The messenger opened the door and called out, "Where's that sick woman?" A voice in another apartment said, "In the next room." He came and said, "Woman, you left your money and things on the center table in the sitting room; here's your money, and I'll just lay your other things on this table here. A lot of fellows came into the sitting room to play cards, and they took your things, money and all, and laid them on the settee. It's a wonder they didn't notice the money, if they had you may bet you never would have seen it again, for I see it's silver or gold. I didn't undo it; you better count it when it gets daylight." I made no reply to this, but he went down muttering to himself — "It's the tarnalest thing in creation that women don't know nothing; they'd better lose their heads and done with it; that would be the thing for 'em to lose." I must say I was heartily glad to hear the voice and clatter of the old man's boots die away in the distance. I now felt relieved, and again dropped into a sound sleep. Morning, noon and night came, and no boat in sight. At last, about two o'clock in the night, or rather in the morning, a sudden rushing noise was heard through the house, and the inmates all seemed to be astir. "A boat in sight!" was heard from below. I sprang to my feet and staggered to the chair which contained our clothes, at the same time awaking my children. We made a speedy toilet and was ready when the proprietor came up with a light, saying that the boat would only touch the wharf. However, he promised to see us on the boat all right. Now all I had to do was to settle my bill. I was led onto the plank and my children carried until we reached the ladies' cabin. Our state room was fitted up splendidly, and we retired immediately to our own room, now of peace and safety. Elizabeth was excited with joy, and the thought of our final escape caused tears of gratitude to flow, as from a newly broken fountain.

Sarah was now fast asleep in her berth, and Elizabeth stood by me, while we thus gave vent to our bursting hearts. We were filled with gratitude to God for the kind care and protection He had manifested to us. The ladies came in to see us; they had been informed that we had made our escape from that infuriated people, the Mormons. This was soon after the assassination of Joseph Smith and others of the leaders of the Mormon church. They asked me several questions, saying they were very anxious to hear something of our history, in that most exciting time among the Mormons. I told them I should at present beg an excuse, as sickness and fatigue would forbid me this pleasure. They then offered to aid me in anything I should wish, and assured me that I need not feel any delicacy in making my wants known to them, as they would most gladly do anything for me and my children. I told them a little rest and quiet would be a great help to us at present. I was very grateful for their kindness; for most truly it made me feel at home and among friends.

The next morning I sent to the clerk's office to pay for my ticket to Cincinnati, Ohio, but the answer came that my ticket was free. When this word came to me, my gratitude was only expressed with tears, as my tongue could not give utterance to what I wished to say.

"What kind of people are those on this boat," thought I; "it must be they are Christians, or they would not bestow so many favors upon us?" That day the ladies came in to see us, and among them was one who told me of her own experience among the Mormons, at which I was surprised. She said her husband had taken another wife, after which she became disgusted and left him and also her property; and he had sold all and gone to Salt Lake City. This lady also said there were three or four more on the boat, who were making their exit from the Mormons, privately though, and consequently kept secluded. Now I felt that I was not alone.

CHAPTER XXII.

The kindness of the people on this boat supplied our every want; even luxuries and dainties were freely dealt out to us both by the captain and the passengers. All seemed to take an interest in our comfort and welfare. I inquired what it all meant. The answer was that I had performed that which six strong men would not dare to undertake, and they considered me worthy of all they could do for me and my children. "He that giveth to the poor, lendeth unto the Lord; and that which he hath given, will He pay him again; good measure, pressed down, shaken together and running over."

The weather continued warm; and as we traveled on, day after day, every day brought us nearer our separation, which I so much dreaded; as I should take another boat at Cincinnati, and should then be separated from those who were so friendly to us. We could not expect this treatment from everyone, and we set this down, not as a general rule, but as an exception. The time arrived for us to change, and when we were about to separate, they handed me seventeen dollars, to be used as I should need it. I shook hands with them, but said not a word, as they carefully helped us on to the next boat. We now were among strangers, and by all appearances, we could not think of finding much sympathy or hospitality. The people appeared different altogether from those on the first boat. A gaming table I noticed in the center of the ladies cabin, and occasionally a set of bloated, red faced men and women seated themselves to take a game of cards. I saw nothing of this among those sensible people on the other boat. One afternoon the card-players assembled and began their merriment, as usual. My children and myself were out now, and had been sitting quietly for some time, resting in easy chairs, when those people came rushing in. They were a lively set, and their merry laughter rang in our ears, which was not in the least agreeable to our throbbing, aching heads. My little girls asked what they were doing. I did not tell them, but caressingly smoothed back their curls, and requested them to lie down upon the sofa. And now they were soon asleep, and as I looked upon them, so pale, so poor, O, how my stricken heart ached for those faithful little creatures. They had wisely kept all I told them in Nauvoo, and in consequence of this we had made our escape safely. I was not able to leave my state room much of the time, only to go to my meals, and this was very seldom. However, in a few days we arrived at Big Beaver, on the Ohio river. Here we took a canal packet to the city of Warren. The cabin maid on this packet was a colored lady and a christian. I received all the attention and care I needed. She attended to our every want with all the promptness of an own mother. I remember the nice dish of blackberries she brought to us, with sugar and cream; I can see just how they looked, although it is now over thirty-five years ago.

We arrived at Warren and went thence to our friends and acquaintances. At this time there were no railroads in this part of the country, and the weary traveler was doomed to sit in a carriage and jolt a long time before he could reach his place of destination. We arrived at our friends after being on the road three weeks, which was then called a quick trip. At this time I was very ill and felt perfectly resigned to pass away and be at rest. We were all safe, and nothing more to fear; but my time had not come; I must struggle on, I had my children to care for. Had it not been for them I would have nothing to care for; but these were all I had left, and if I had not these, what would I have to care for in this world? I have thought, at times, when the air castles were being erected in my imagination, which would glisten with the magnificence of Solomon's temple; the anticipation of which would gild the picture of them, when they should become young women, and companionship should be enjoyed, and pride crown my old age, that they are my children whom I have reared through much care and suffering, for the world to admire. How many mothers, think you, have had the same hope? and how many, think you, have had those hopes crushed to the ground, and their aged heads brought down with sorrow to the grave? The culture of children can be improved; but where there are children there needs also be wealth, in order to rear them properly and approvingly. They can be taught, even in infancy, the Lord's prayer, and in after years the meaning of the words. They can also be taught how to act toward other children. They can learn how to mind their parents and to reverence old people, and how to be pleasant and courteous. Nothing looks better than this; it is something which every one admires. This is one great secret — courtesy will pave your way with pebbles of gold all along life's path, removing thorns and thistles, and will make soft your pillow at night. Teach your children courtesy, and they have an armor which will win the victory over almost any obstacle in life. But I have wandered strangely from my story. My strength was fast failing, and I had become so weak I could not speak above a whisper. My physician told me there was no hopes of my recovery; that he would do all he could, but the case was not in any manner an encouraging one; however, if the weather became cool there might possibly be a little better prospect. My choice, whether to live or die was a matter of little consequence to me. Had it not been for my family I should have chosen rather to go and be at rest; but my time had not come, and my work was not accomplished. I was still more convinced that my days were not numbered when reading the first verses which met my observation on opening the bible, which were as follows: "The right hand of the Lord is exalted. The right hand of the Lord doeth valiantly. I shall not die, but shall live and declare the works of the Lord. The Lord hath chastened me sore, but He hath not given me over unto death." I closed the book, and now felt an assurance that I should get well; and telling my nurse, who was a christian lady, that I should recover, I referred her to the book of Psalms, 118th chapter, 16th, 17th and 18th verses. She read the verses and replied that it was a very singular paragraph for me to open to just then, and very appropriate too; but I saw that she doubted the assurance which I cherished; this lady was my nurse, but not matronly, she was only twenty years of age, and very amiable. However, I perceived that a change was taking place. Howbeit, my friends were incredulous in regard to my surviving the period of two days at the longest, and as they took me in their arms and carrid me into another apartment where it would be more convenient to lay me out, I should have laughed if I had not been too weak, for I knew just what it meant; but I did not believe it would turn out as they thought. Nevertheless, I was perfectly willing that they should enjoy their own opinion if that would be any satisfaction.

My little girls had recovered and gone to live with good people in the vicinity where my friends resided. My recovery was slow, but at the close of every week I found myself a little better; and six long months elapsed before I could call myself free from this horrible fever. I look back upon the period with perfect dread. I am sometimes half persuaded to believe that satan himself had a hand in the whole transaction. Read Job, 11th chapter, 6th verse: " And the Lord said unto Satan, ' Behold, he is in thine hand, but save his life.' " I have also thought sometimes that I was smitten with the fever that I might not make my escape with my children from the danger which awaited us. However, I had now recovered enough to sit up a little, and within a few weeks could help myself more and more.

now was compelled to endure a rumor which was set afloat upon the wings of the wind, by that most hateful thing called malice — a rumor which had been freshly manufactured and presented to those who are ever ready to "roll a lie as a sweet morsel under their tongue," and seeming to relish it the better if they could only obtain it before the agreeable odor of fire and brimstone had passed off, and the smell of the bottomless pit. This odor and taste were sweeter to them than honey in the honey comb. Who was he that said: " Blessed are ye when men shall revile you and shall persecute you, and shall say all manner of evil against you falsely, for My sake. Rejoice and be exceeding glad, for great is your reward in heaven; for so persecuted they the prophets which were before you? This was He who suffered death for us, and can we not bear a little reproach for His sake? for the eyes of the Lord are over the righteous, and His ears are open unto their prayers; but the face of the Lord is against them that do evil; and who is he that will harm you if ye be followers of that which is good? And if ye suffer for righteousness sake, happy are ye. Be not afraid of their terror; neither be troubled, having a good conscience, that whereas they speak evil of you as of evil doers, they may be ashamed that falsely accuse your good conversation in Christ."— 1 Peter, 3: 12, 13, 14, 16. Therefore, having the blessed assurance that happily I was Christ's, and that He was mine, this assurance raised me far above and beyond the vain and transitory things of this sinful world; I could rest peacefully on His blessed promises, and look away to that beautiful home prepared for the poor, weary pilgrim, by the Savior's own hand. That same hand will smooth our dying pillow, and wipe away all tears from our eyes. How sweet the words — "Come, ye blessed of my Father, inherit the kingdom prepared for you."

CHAPTER XXIII.

My time at the millinery table was as well improved as my feeble strength would allow; but the thought of being separated from my family almost destroyed my reason. At night, in my wakeful hours, I have asked myself these questions: "Have they comfortable places to sleep? Do they fare as well as they would with me, or are they neglected, and no one to care for them? O, God, protect and take care of them." Then the thought came that if I trusted in Him, my children should not suffer. I had one consolation, and that was,

> "We would not live always, I ask not to stay
> Where storm after storm rises dark o'er the way."

No, we like all others were passing away, and in a few days, perhaps years, if we are patient, we shall join that happy company who have passed through the furnace of affliction, and have been purified as gold is purified in the furnace. This was a very great trial, which required a special degree of grace and firmness.

I now was called upon to attend a family who were all sick; I think there was not one exempt. I called the next day and found a house resembling a hospital. I told them I would do for them the best in my power, but they had chosen a poor nurse, I feared. But they were glad of even my assistance. We concluded it was caused by something they had eaten; they were covered with boils. "We are dreadfully afflicted," said the lady, "and would be glad of your assistance. Did the little boy tell you what our illness was?" inquired the lady. "Yes, he said you were all covered over with boils." The lady smiled and said the family were all on beds, some in one place and some in another, above and below; "and for three days and nights we have had no rest," she said. "Go where you will, there is a couch and sick child, and I am tired out, but have to watch the baby" (pointing to a bed room); "they are quiet now for the first time, the mercy knows how long. Now if you will help us through," said the good lady, "I will be very grateful indeed; furthermore, you shall be well remunerated for your trouble." "O, I will not refuse; some one must help you, that is apparent," I said. And suiting my actions to my words, feeling that I had a duty before me, I commenced the work, to do by others as I would have them do by me under like circumstances.

The time passed off much more agreeable than any one would dare imagine, and three weeks told the story. I was free once more, and returned to my boarding place with the satisfaction that I had done my duty. During the latter part of summer I made arrangements to again commence keeping house. I informed Mrs. E. of the fact, to which she objected, saying she could not think of my leaving her. "You have been with us over a year, and seem like one of our own family, and you can remain with us as long as you live for that matter." Of course, I too would not wish to leave; but after one has had a home of their own they realize its comforts. "Ah, remember," said Mrs. E., "you had some one then to provide for that home. However, it is perfectly natural and right; but you will find it more difficult to get along than you now do; and another thing, your health is not by any means sufficient to maintain your family and pay all expenses. You have lost sight of the many difficulties which attends housekeeping. In fact, it is easy to think, but hard to do," Mrs. E. said. "We find, too, that it is easy to be a fair-weather christian, bold where there is nothing to be done, and confident where there is nothing to be feared; difficulties unmask him to others; temptations unmask him to himself. He discovers that although he is a professor he is no christian." "Mrs. E., your argument is good," I said; "but still I have a mind to try it, and if I do not succeed, which truly I may not, it will be no more than others have done." "True," she replied, "but like a brave soldier who is supported under dangers by a strong faith, that the fruits of that victory for which he is fighting will be safety, peace and glory; but alas, the pleasures of this life are present and visible; the honors are remote for which he is striving; he therefore fails because nothing short of a lively faith can ever outweigh a strong present temptation, and lead one to prefer joys of conquest to the pleasures of indulgence." "Well, Mrs. E., your council is answered in few words; that you almost convince me of my weakness in judgment concerning this matter. And yet I can truly say that if there is anything contrary to the code of wisdom and good judgment, the dictates of which I should be tempted to follow, it would most assuredly be that of having a snug little home of my own. But Providence has taken away every means of my earthly support, and my nature is in opposition to His decree. Nothing can ever reconcile me to my loss but the special grace of God."

Again, when I meditate that this was a divine appointment, my murmurings are not uttered; I would drive them from my inmost thoughts when desires come like the love of a pleasant home, and when we cannot see the faintest shadow of harm, we are most likely to bring it about, even if it is in a temporary structure, or some form which could answer in part our inmost desires, and thus alleviate our sorrows, and for a time beguile the realities of misfortunes. I therefore rented rooms of Mr.

A., and with the assistance of my oldest daughter prepared for a removal. Mr. and Mrs. E. loaded the wagon with necessaries for housekeeping, the same as for an own daughter, and tears ran down their withered cheeks as they were loading the team for my departure. They were old people and quite gray, and if ever my heart ached for any people beside my own parents, it was for them. However, I told them they would now have a place to visit, which they readily agreed to. Those people were highly respected. Mr. E. was educated for the ministry, and had been in public business in his young days, and Mrs. E. was a Friend — a Quaker in her religious views, but did not use the Quaker phrases. While I remained with them, I became acquainted with their children, who were leading men and women in the higher ranks of society. One of their daughters was in long membership with the M. E. church in E. V., to which I had joined as a probationer, and afterward joined in full membership. This was in Espyville, Pa., in the year 1847. In our little quiet home we passed many happy days and hours, and were not neglected by those good old people, Mr. and Mrs. Espy. Our stay at this place was only about two or three years. I had procured homes for some of my children where they intended stopping permanently, as my health, it was evident, would never be sufficient to maintain them. I had a severe attack of rheumatism, and being necessarily under medical treatment, I was compelled to abandon all hopes of ever procuring a home for myself and children, as I had sometimes fancied I could. My place in Nauvoo would not make a home for us unless the taxes were kept paid up. At this period my health had become very much impaired with hard labor and exposure, through wet and cold, and fatigue of getting a living. Impaired and disabled, I was still under medical treatment, I did not slacken my vigilance, working on early and late, and at times working all night in order to fill my engagements — although this is nothing unusual for any who follow sewing for a livelihood.

At the time of which I am writing, my daughter Nellie was with me most of the time; a small portion of the time she spent with friends four miles away. She was a splendid child, both in looks and in behavior. She was fourteen and was ambitious, frugal and tidy. My oldest son, William, was now ten; a very promising, smart little boy, very quiet, though full of merriment and attractiveness. My two sons were in their infancy brought very low with illnes, even to the verge of the grave, but were raised through much care and watchfulness. I thought, at the time of which I now write, they all had as good places as could be found, and I tried to think the people with whom I had entrusted them would do the fair thing by them. But there is no torture so cruel as for a mother to be separated from her children; however hard this may be, many a mother has been under the necessity of enduring this thorn in her side during her natural life.

In this little home we still lingered. Sometimes we could get what was necessary, but when the snow was deep we could not get enough for our comforts; but the rain never hindered us; we could go through mud and rain to get work, and take it home when finished. In a small village work must be done cheaply, and consequently a great deal of work must be done for a little money. House rent must be paid, wood must be got and cut fire length, and paid for, besides clothing and all other necessaries of life must be had. Notwithstanding all the difficulties under which we were laboring, I can truly say, as King David, " I had rather be a door-keeper in the house of God than to dwell in the tents of wickedness. I was away from the Mormons, and my children were safe too. I ought never to complain a word about anything more as long as I live; it seems wicked. God had done so much for us, placed us among christians, and a people who respect the law; people who regard morality, and chastity, and virtue; people who are charitable to the unfortunate, and were engaging their utmost powers to subdue evil and promote good, and to crush out wickedness and build up righteousness. These were the people among whom we dwelt; and this being the case, what had we to fear?

I received a letter from my mother, who then resided in Wisconsin, requesting me to come to her; that she could cure me, she thought. But not having strength to undergo the journey, I resolved on going to my brother's in Meadville, as two of my brothers resided in that place, which was only twenty miles distant. Here I probably should abide until I recovered from my painful disease, the rheumatism. The journey, though a short one, was productive of a long siege of utter helplessness, and I could not be moved in bed for the time of three weeks. However, after this period, I began to mend; and received another letter from my mother to come to Wisconsin as soon as I should be able to travel; but as there was no railroad as yet from Meadville to Erie, I abandoned all hopes of getting out to Madison, Wisconsin, for some length of time. As soon as I was able to get about again I commenced work in a millinery establishment with Mrs. Vincent — a large emporium of millinery and dress goods — and remained there throughout the business part of the winter season, through which term my brother's house was filled with boarders, students of the Allegheney College; and through the summer season also, this house was the students' home.

Notwithstanding my brother's manifestation of his desire that I should remain with him until I should permanently regain my health, I had a great desire to again see my dear old mother, and acknowledge to her by word how sorry I had always felt for leaving home and going with the Mormons; that I truly believed this illness and misfortune was all caused by doing that which I knew was contrary to the wishes of my parents. I therefore conducted my affairs to suit this resolve as properly as my ability would allow, and agreeable to this conclusion I started in the stage for Erie, it being thirty miles from Meadville. I said I started, but the stage coach stood before the door in patient waiting; for a number of our friends had assembled early at my brother's to bid me farewell, and the delay was caused by the many tears and good wishes and cautions to take good care of myself. These were they who were in the serenade under the window the night previous. The music was lovely, and the words magnificent and applicable; beautiful as the splendor and stillness of night. After the door of the coach was opened and I had found a seat, each one of those ladies came and presented their card, and after the compliment was returned and the farewells repeated, we were speedily whirled away. A long sigh was a short rest to me, as the stage drove up to a watering trough, and the passengers had one after another alighted upon the platform in front of a hotel; but it was a sigh of relief. They had all left the stage in order to get straightened out and rested. An old gentleman and myself were now the only occupants, and as this old gentleman noticed the sigh which almost unconsciously escaped my lips, he said: "Madam, are you ill?" "Yes, I have been afflicted some time with rheumatism," I replied. "Poor mortal," said the good old gentleman, while tears of pity and compassion filled his eyes. Sure enough, thought I, if any one upon this earth needs pity, I think it is me. However, within a few moments the passengers returned, and I again was compelled to cramp myself up into close quarters, and remain in the same position until I arrived at a hotel in Erie. On reaching there my sufferings were great, and I almost abandoned the idea of taking a boat the morning following. That night at the hotel was one long to be remembered. I was tortured with pain from head to foot, and with much difficulty I managed to keep my groans to myself, without disturbing the inmates. However, the morning came at last, and with the morning came bitter memories of the necessity I was under to leave those loved ones, and seek relief at the hands of my mother yet so far away.

This was the first time I had ever seen Lake Erie in the summer, and a steamboat on the lake, under sail, did not look larger than a small bird flying in the air. I started the next morning for Detroit, Michigan, and after a stormy night and the horrors of being buried in the deep, we finally landed in Detroit about daylight. I had received a card while at Erie, for the "Johnson House," saying all baggage carried free to and from the landing. After arriving at the house the proprietor came and said I had better get my baggage checked, and also directed me to the depot, which I immediately attended to. This was something which I was not accustomed to, for as yet I had never seen a car, and consequently had this all to learn. After getting my baggage checked I met the drayman as I was going into the ladies sitting room, who accosted me with this: "Fifty cents, madam, for bring up your baggage." "I am stopping at the Johnson House, and my card tells me that all baggage is carried free to and from the landing." "Can't help that; I shall take your goods if you don't pay." I paid no attention to this; but after this the baggage-master had to interpose, else he would have taken my goods. At half past five the passengers began to assemble at the depot, and at six P. M. I was on my way to Milwaukee, after which I arrived at my mothers, in or near Madison. This was a journey long to be remembered; however, the satisfaction of seeing my mother and sisters was indescribable, and I will not attempt it at this time.

I remained at my mother's until my health had so far recovered that I considered myself almost as well as ever, and I went to work at my trade in the city of Madison. Having learned that my beloved sister Jane was living at Fond du Lac, I immediately wrote her of my arrival. I had not seen this favorite sister since we joined in girlish glee at our own father's fireside; yet our correspondence never had been relinquished, and the same sisterly affection still remained, pure as when our little feet wandered together in woodlands sweetest bower, to see the murmuring streamlet or listen to the charmingly sweet songsters of the fresh, green forest, which re-echoed the clapping of our hands and merry voices, at some unexpected joy of the newly discovered curiosities. The friendship still remained just as pure as then, and in reply to my letter I received the following answer:

"My Dear Sister:—Do visions of a dream, in hours of slumber, again occupy my anxious mind? or do messengers of winged ones revisit the hours of midnight flattering a heart swelled with hope and despair, when accents in soft whispers have said to me, "You shall see her again before death closes the scene." Those dreams and thoughts have filled my anxious mind since you, my dear sister, left me. I cannot tell now how I spent my time after being bereft of your society; no other one at home whom I could substitute for your loss. Seeking the society of others only added grief to disappointment. My walks were lonely and disconsolate; I was like a dove who mourned her absent mate. I often absented myself from the family to seek meditation, and resorted to the hills or groves, or sought a spreading tree. There I would seat myself, and the times when you were with me would crowd upon my memory, and for a time fanciful ideas have magnified realities, until coming to myself as awaking from a pleasant dream.

> The melody of a summer breeze,
> The thrilling notes of birds,
> Can never be so dear to me
> As your remembered words.

I sought a balm for a wounded spirit in various ways. The merry and giddy dance — I sought it there, but found it not. I often took my little book as a companion; not the novelties of a character of benighted merits, which had hitherto been my refuge, but one which may well be called a cordial for every wounded spirit. This blessed history, the Hero of which is of such a character, so full of pity, whose eyes are ever moved, and whose ear is never turned, nor His arm ever shortened, this is the companion I now chose; and from that happy moment I have found Him to be all I could wish or desire, or worthy to receive. Years have, however, found me the mother of a family, and I am aware that this period of my life is to me ot the greatest importance; I realize the need of a well fortified mind.

I have wandered far from what I wished first to say; it is this: Can it be that my own dearest sister is in Madison, and we shall meet again? This was what filled my mind when I read your welcome letter. You may look for me the first of November, if you remain there. I will try to wait until I see you; and for the present, farewell. J. H."

I will not attempt here to describe my feelings on reading this letter. My feeble language would fail at the attempt should I try to tell what sad forebodings of the past were now presented to my memory. I little thought how firmly her affections were placed on me. She had repeatedly written me, yet she never had expressed her feelings so plainly as now; and my heart was torn asunder, and that not undeservingly, either, for I felt that I had thoughtlessly forfeited true happiness for an uncertain reward of peace and satisfaction, when the tide of rewards should come in. Alas! the time had passed and gone forever; I could not recall the days and years which might have been spent with her and given comfort to her most noble heart. However just or unjust may be the cause of our separation, I must leave this to be decided in the unknown future; and now I must suffer remorse for doing what I truly thought at the time would be acceptable in the sight of God. "He that loveth father or mother, brother or sister, house or land, more than Me, is not worthy of me." These are the words of our blessed Savior; and for fear I should be found to fight against God's works, I left my home and friends and went with the deluded Mormon church, from whom I could not obtain a surety for a peaceful or a glorious victory or reward at last. But here I leave this story and contemplate the visit from my sister in person.

The time at length arrived when she intended to come to Madison. It had rained for three days and nights; the streets were all in a complete float of water, and not a person could be seen upon the sidewalks. Whenever I cast a glance at the deplorable condition of the weather, all I could see to gladden me was the large letters on the "Argus" printing office. "What is it that a printer cannot do?" thought I; they can make fair weather when it rains; they make one smile through a tear; they can turn winter into summer, and thorns and thistles into fresh roses and beautiful flowers; they can make a poor man rich; they can create friends and subdue enemies; they can build up or pull down;

they can make pleasant homes; they can make your life happy and agreeable — yes, they can do this and much more. I cannot enumerate all they can do, thought I to myself as I turned from the window against which the rain was dashing furiously. And now I was seated again at the work table, and forgetful of the time my poor sister would have if she had started just before this unmerciful rain. No doubt she laid by for the rain to subside.

The next morning it was still raining; and after the usual routine of housework was accomplished, as also my toilet, I was standing at the front window, and all I could see was "Argus" office, looking earnestly to catch a glimpse, or a transitory object of a cheerful nature, to drive dull cares away, for it was one of those dismal days which makes one feel like one forsaken. I was viewing the awful condition of the roads and the prospect of traveling; thinking of my sister, and saying to myself, " O, dear, it always does rain when I am in any great expectation about anything;" when suddenly a carriage drove up to my door. It was now pouring rain. I concluded they were coming in a moment to find a shelter from the storm. The driver immediately alighted, and hurriedly throwing open the carriage door, a young, good looking lady stepped out, and a hurried rap was heard at the front door. I led the way into a warm, comfortable apartment, and asked her to lay off her damp cloak and hat; but she said they would go again soon; and after a brief conversation about the rain, and she had surveyed me closely, she inquired: "Are you sister to Mrs. Hulce?—Jane Hulce, I mean." "Yes, I am her sister; or at least I have a sister by that name." "Well," said the young lady, "she is out at aunt's, in the country; I am her daughter, and have come after you." "O, heaven; is that possible?" I exclaimed. "Is this Jane's own daughter; my abused, poor sister whom I left, to go off with the Mormons?" This was what filled my mind as this came from the beautiful lips of Jane's own daughter, Nettie Hulce; and in less time than I am writing this, I was in the carriage, whirling along through mud and water. It was eight miles travel. However, we reached the abode of Adeline Butterfield, and my sister Jane and I were in each other's arms. I tried to speak, but it was not possible. I tried again, but could not utter a word; if I could have spoken, they would have been words of repentence. She understood all, but said not a word. · If we could have spoken, I should have said: "Can you forgive me?"

and her answer would have been a four-fold acquittance, right from her heart, too. Twenty long, weary years had passed since we separated at our father's house. In vain we tried to find words to communicate our satisfaction and thankfulness to meet once more; but we soon found that tears were a far better substitute than the deficient English language.

After all, our visit was a sober one; we were both willing it should be; memories of the past had so gathered around our hearts, it really seemed cruel to even smile; consequently, our meeting was attended with sobriety. The rain had now subsided, and only now and then a cloud could be seen. The next morning we arose to once more inhale the fresh atmosphere. O, how unsurpassingly delightful, to once more take a stroll in this newly washed herbage and air, with my own dear sister. The herbage, however, was a second growth of grass and flowers on the prairie, as the frost had turned the most early herbage to a dark redish hue. The breeze seemed to blow for the self same purpose, to accommodate our wishes, and gave us strength and life. We were now wrapped together in that sweetest of all love, that of which the Savior said, "See that ye love one another fervently."

CHAPTER XXIV.

In the year 1855, we consigned our mother and sister and her husband to the grave. The small-pox had caused mortality to reign in our midst, and taken those who were dear to us, and now only two sisters remained in the vicinity of Madison. One of those was Mrs. M. A. Cook, wife of Dr. J. Cook, who was president of Dane county poor house. After my mother's death I removed to Bellevue, Iowa, as at this time my oldest daughter had married and came to that place with my two sons, expecting to make that their permanent home. After my arrival there, and finding there was no milliner in the place, I commenced the work, determined on making it a success. I therefore thought to use caution, not as yet knowing what the result would be. My work increased, and I may well say the prospect looked promising. I now found myself with a large run of custom, and had reason to fancy that my work was appreciated by all. This was a great satisfaction indeed. Money was plenty, and all business in a flourishing condition; and finding it necessary to procure help, I engaged a young lady milliner to assist in the business, having all I could do attending to orders and the many wants which were proclaimed in my ears every hour in the day. Applications to take apprentice girls were not in the least uncommon, and this afforded me a chance to take my choice. I stocked my store in small bills in the commencement, until I was overrun with as many solicitations for things I had not got as there is hours in business, and consequently I procured an assortment to accommodate if possible all demands of my worthy patrons. I filled up my store; my income increased far beyond my expectations and continued good for a number of years.

One morning I received a call from two young ladies just from England, applying to me for a place as apprentices. I did not need but one to fill a vacancy, and it was decided that the oldest should come. I soon learned by her that she only wished to stay three or four weeks and then set up the business for themselves. I must say I was not a little surprised at this, and concluded for that short period I could not afford to be very particular in teaching her all the trade. She informed me that her sister would join with her; also that they had a legacy, and they wished to put it to the best use possible; and believing the millinery a business by which they could more than double their money within a short time, they concluded they could not be too soon in availing themselves of this golden opportunity. I told them their mistake; that they would do better to put their money out at interest than to invest it in millinery goods and try to sell them in Bellevue to double their capital; but they did not listen to my selfish whim. They knew better than all that; and very soon they had a host of choice, costly goods put up in their shop window in a style more befitting London than our small village. Their management plainly showed their lack of knowledge in the business, the need of which they found when too late, and the fruits of which were sure to send them back to their own country without a penny at their journey's end.

At the end of six months I visited them. As I entered, I saw at a glance that their continuance was that of troubled anxiety. After a brief conversation of an indifferent character, I inquired how they prospered in business. They told me they had sold just enough to know that one-fourth of the money which they thought could be made was not realized by them as yet, and unless they could do better for six months to come than they had done, they would give up the trade and willingly seek some other employment for their money and their hands; but now the main part of their goods were yet on the shelf, and they must dispose of them in some shape. They told me they had no one to blame but themselves for not falling in with my advice in this matter. They had, in the short period of six months, lost six hundred dollars.

Another year told the story. They lost all except just enough to defray the expenses of one of them to England. The other was soon married and in domestic employment. Those young ladies were handsome and pleasant, also industrious, but did not understand finance in America, and probably not in their own country, for they were young and inexperienced. This is no wonder, for many who are older and more experienced Americans do not keep clear from difficulties of a far more serious nature than the one I have just named. However, I mention this as one of the events within my experience, not as anything uncommon or wonderful; but it perhaps might be a profit to those who are about to take a step in any kind of speculation, to "look before they leap."

At this time I was surprised also to find a discontinuance in my own custom; money more scarce, and people generally were talking about hard times. State banks were failing; and finally a regular money panic ensued, which was not at this time groundless. The caution about trading was apparent. Clerks went to sleep on the counter at all business places, or else devotedly pressed into some entangled love story. For some time I did not know how things would turn out, knowing all who were in business would suffer loss. My business was in a shape which gave me trouble, although it was not a great amount; but a few hundred dollars was more than I was willing my creditors should lose by me. They came to see me, but it was not possible to pay them with the money I had; and after trying to sell what I had to raise the money, I also failed in that. I therefore wrote to them saying they could take the goods at the price they charged me, and then endorse the same on my note, which was satisfactory to both parties. I felt relieved and willing to owe less for goods, and do a small business at such a time as this.

CHAPTER XXV.

After the care and burden of having so much on my hands had settled into a small compass, which made it more in accordance with the demand of this embarrassing time, and hard labor was both capital and interest, I still had the comfort of having my children, all except one, near me. My oldest daughter was married, and my oldest son was only five miles in the country, with a rich old farmer, Captain Potter, at which place he remained until the commencement of the civil war, in 1861. My youngest son remained with me, and found employment in a steam lath mill, for which he received one dollar per day. He was now thirteen years of age, and his wages amounted to twenty-six dollars per month. The gentleman for whom he worked was Thomas Hays, a worthy citizen of Bellevue. My daughter Elizabeth remained with her sister Nellie for some time, after which she returned to Ohio, and shortly after was married.

The subject of Mormonism had not as yet ever been mentioned to my youngest children, nor had I ever, under any circumstances, named to them the sad event that I ever had any knowledge of them. Those of my family who were of an age to know something about it were repeatedly cautioned in regard to revealing this secret to anyone. With much caution I managed to keep this from the public, until of late I have felt it my duty to let it be known, that the public may beware of the leaders of Salt Lake Mormons in particular. There are some very good people among them I do not deny; but the ground work is dangerous. By experience I know what their principles were before they left Illinois to go to Salt Lake; these principles they took with them, and they have been carried out, to all intents and purposes. I know their schemes, and how they make use of God's word to carry out their dark designs and purposes. The Book of Mormon is said to contain a history of old prophets who came to this continent in an early age. Their names were Nephi, Laman, Mormon, Lemuel, Lehi and Sam. It appears by this Book of Mormon that the Lord commanded those men to build a boat and cross the big waters; and as they were building the craft the Lord told them how it should be built; that there should be a hold in the top thereof and a hold in the bottom thereof, and the boat was to be round.

This is the way they journeyed to this goodly land, that flows with milk and honey. The Mormons say that the Indians are descendants of Laman, and Nephi was the son of Laman. I think I am not mistaken, although it has been a great many years since 1 saw the Book of Mormon; however, I think I am correct. The Indians are called Lamonites by all the Mormons, and the white people who do not believe in the Mormons are called Gentiles, or Pagans. The Mormons believe firmly, too, that the Lamonites will tread down the Gentiles, for they say the mouth of the Lord hath spoken it. They also say that when they are of a sufficient number they will help the Lamonites tread down the wicked Pagans, or Gentiles. As their numbers increase their hearts no doubt rejoice, thinking of the time when victory shall be won. Being numerous, and their number continually increasing, they expect one day to overthrow this republic. This has long since been in the minds of the Latter Day Saints, and it is no mistake of the writer. I have heard this talked of and preached by the Saints and Elders of the church, time after time. It is no wonder that polygamy has been introduced among the Salt Lake Mormons, pretending as they do that they have a perfect right to serve God according to the dictates of their own conscience; and this is according to the constitution of our government. They pretend that this is a revelation from God, and also a command of God; and to increase their number they are not in the least backward about obeying this command; also pretending that this is according to the will of God and the laws of the land. Polygamy was not practiced until the Mormons were driven out of Missouri, and their compelled exodus from their possessions aroused in them such indignation towards the government that rebellion filled every Mormon's heart. But concerning the Lamonites treading down the Gentiles, I often heard this spoken of: "For," said they, "the Indians have been driven from their homes and hunting grounds, and we have shared the same; and the time will come, brethren, when they will wade in blood up to their horses bridles. We have petitioned to government for redress, but they have refused to grant our petition; we have suffered, brethren and sisters, often suffered with cold and hunger, and weariness; driven from our homes and quiet firesides, we have been smitten, buffeted, despised, tormented and hated; we wandered in wet and cold, without shelter or friends, law or justice; we have sought our own but it was denied us. Heaven demands justice, but it is still refused. May God hasten his work; may judgment follow our appressors."

This is what I have heard repeatedly from the Mormon elders, while they were preaching on the Sabbath day. It is not according to the gospel of Christ, which says, "Whosoever shall smite thee on the right cheek, turn to him the other also; and if any man will sue thee at the law and take away thy coat, let him have thy cloak also. Love your enemies; bless them that curse you; do good to them that hate you, and pray for them that despitefully use you and persecute you; for he maketh the sun to shine on the evil and on the good, and sendeth rain on the just and on the unjust." And still I have something to say in favor of these people. One thing is, they are industrious and frugal, and very cleanly; cleanliness with the Mormons is Christ-like. They preach this also from the Book of Covenants. This book is also said to be a revealed work of God, through Joseph Smith, the Mormon prophet. The Book of Commandments is likewise called a revelation from God. The Book of Covenants and that of Revelations compose one book, although in two volumes; and by those books the Mormon church is governed. A committe is elected by the church for the purpose of visiting each family, in order to ascertain how their houses are kept, and if any filth exists. When each house is thoroughly searched, the committee orders the filth, if any is found, speedily removed; and if it is not attended to before their next visit, those members are reported to higher authorities. Every house is visited each week by the committee, and a thorough examination is made. Door yards, in the summer time, are also examined, and all uncleanliness speedily eradicated and buried deep with fresh earth. This is to arrest disease by timely antecedence. This order is strictly kept up, whether in the city or otherwise. In each ward is a committee appointed, and those rules are strictly and cautiously adhered to. All clothing must likewise be kept clean and sweet, and children are not allowed to be seen in the street with uncombed heads or unwashed faces. Their clothing also must be made with taste and elegance, and kept perfectly tidy.

The Mormons have two other books besides the Book of Mormon, or in other words, as it is sometimes called, the Mormon Bible; the Words of Wisdom and their hymn book. These constitute the whole number of books by which they worship and are governed. Their children are baptized at the age of eight years. Their form of baptism is immersion, and no other way is allowed to be baptism. The rules of the church prohibit eating meat except on special occasions, namely: at a feast or social gathering or a wedding, and then to eat very sparing. At those amusements they are allowed to have wine, but this must be of their own manufacture, of the pure juice of the grape. No coffee or tea is allowed to be used, as they are taught in the Word of Wisdom that hot drinks are not good for man. But I must change the subject for the present.

It was now a time to see sober faces; all business was suspended; almost every person who was depending on day labor for their support carried with them a sad countenance. Add to this there was but little demand for the production of manufacturers in many business houses; the winters were long and severe, and it seemed impossible for poor people to subsist upon the small pittance they received for a day's labor. If even they were so lucky as to obtain a day's work, how gratefully the sum of fifty cents a day was received by the poor laborer. However, spring came at last, bringing with it, as it always does, bright and fresh courage, and I again resumed my accustomed occupation, the straw millinery. I could by this keep clear from debt and pay my expenses, although the work was hard and difficult, which is always the case in this business. I still kept the colored girl, and dismissed all the other help, except now and then an assistant for a day or two. Refinishing was the orders of each day, as my customers would say money was too scarce to allow them to purchase new materials. My pressing was accomplished by hand, as it would not answer the purpose to press so many different shapes with a pressing machine, which was not adequate for this purpose; and as my work was done in the upper part of a drug store, I found it not only hard but inconvenient. I therefore thought to make a little alteration in the arrangement, which would be lessening the trouble of doing my bleaching in rainy weather. I knew of a room which had not been opened or occupied since I came into the house, and for years before probably, and on examination I found the fastening only consisted of a nail put in tightly over the latch, and with my scissors I drew it out, and the door came open as if by magic. I entered, and the odor nearly overcame me; the atmosphere was stifling. This was owing to its having had no ventilation. In one corner there was an old barrel, straw and litter of every kind, an old pair of rusty tongs, and a huge looking bench in the center. I was thinking I would have Jane come and clean the apartment at once. " But look here," said my boy, who was examining the contents of the barrel, "here is something tied up in a rag." "Put that right down, I beseech you," said I as we stepped to the door. It was a private room for dissectieg dead bodies. This so frightened my son that he ran to Jane exclaiming, "Jane, Jane, there are ghosts in that room!" I found it impossible to pacify either my son or the black girl. They declared they would not stay in the house one night. I tried to get Jane to promise to stay with me one night, but she said she would not; and to use her own words, she said: " Now Miss, mark my word, if ye stay heah you'll suffer de consequence, now I tell ye. I stay heah? no, no; I stay in no ghost house; mebbe some dese dark nights you'll be missin' in de mornin'. Now listen, Miss; dese fellers jes lib bile ye up as look at ye, dat's what's de mattah; dey hab no princ'pl wat eber, now I tell ye, Miss," and her countenance was so earnestly expressive of her fear, that if I had been sure her suggestions had been true, I should have laughed heartily to see her expression. I told her we had not been molested and there was no more danger now than there was before the room was opened. "Nonsense, Jane; it is not worth thinking about." "Well, Miss," she replied, "I tell ye dar was jes' much danga afore de do was open, only we dono it afo; but now lem me tell ye, if ye don git out ob dis house somethin' will apeah som ob dese dark nights, an' ye'll wish ye was dun gon in som safe place, and mebbe dey'll kill ye rite off."

With much difficulty I prevailed on those frightened creatures to remain with me one night. We retired that night feeling quite composed, to all appearance, and I felt comforted when I heard from each bed a sound sleeping breathing, which reminded me that all was well. I too, soon forgot my trouble. This slumber was not long enjoyed, however, for if half of the house had broken down it could not have made more racket than that which brought us to our feet. The lamp was lighted by a trembling hand, and my little boy and Jane were almost breathless. The noise was in the back hall. We could do no more than to go into the millinery room, and after fastening each door securely and turning down the lamp, we spent the night talking and wondering what that crashing noise could mean. The next day, however, I noticed that the human bones in the barrel in the mysterious room had all disappeared. Here I will pause, and go back. The noise we heard in the hall was remote from the mysterious room, being entirely on the opposite side of the building. My impression was that some one had broken the door down in the hall, which I had always kept bolted, as soon as dark, and as we came out of our bed rooms I intended to unlock the inside hall door and see what had happened. I bade my son to take some kind of a weapon, a stick of wood or a flat-iron, and when I opened the door he must throw it with all his might; the stick was in his hand, upraised, and I unlocked the door, while the white of Jane's eyes and half-opened mouth, showed plainly of her wonderful terror; she almost breathlessly begged me not to open the door, for, said she, "you have opened one door, and see what trouble it made." My hand was on the door nob and my son stood ready to throw, while Jane uttered those words. Finally my courage failed, and I quickly locked the door again, and spent the night in the millinery department. But I hear some one say, "Yes, that is just like a woman, they cannot rest a moment without investigating; yes, every nook and corner must be criticised, and thorough work made in the examination, too." This charge, I, for one, do not deny; and if luckily there is one who does deny this, it is not a woman; they inherit this disposition from Mother Eve. Father Adam also had propensities, that is, to lay all the blame to God and his wife when he transgressed, saying, "The woman whom Thou gavest to be with me, she gave me of the tree and I did eat." That day I was left alone, for before the setting of the sun both Jane and my boy had deserted the premises of the ghost department.

I was now left to myself to think over the past, and wonder why something good could never come into my life's pathway; some cheering ray to gild the rough landscape which now lay stretched out before my saddened spirit. After a little hasty walk, I prevailed on a maiden lady of my acquaintance to accompany me for a short time until I could arrange my business differently, and change my situation; but as Miss Linn was engaged to teach, she could not agree to stay for any definite period, but would gladly stay as long as circumstances would allow; but as she could not be my company that present evening, I was obliged to spend the night solitary and alone. It was intensely warm weather; I consequently raised the windows, and the paper curtains were moved by the quiet breeze in such a manner as to remind one of a person struggling for breath; and it sounded so perfectly heinous to me that sleep entirely left my eyelids, and I once more rejoiced to see the dawn of another day. To change my place of residence was now my greatest desire, and to this purpose I directed every faculty; and in this period I should have the pleasure of Miss Linn's society, which now I knew so well how to prize. "Then you are surely going away?" she said, the morning she entered my room. "Yes, I think of going," I said, "but don't know how soon." "Pray tell me," said she, "where you think of going." "Well," I answered, "I have not mentioned that to any but one, and that is my daughter." "O, yes," she replied; "she must dread to part with you." "Of course she does," I said; "but what can a person do in such a place as this? I depend on working at my trade for a living, and if I can't get that to do, what can I do? You know I am not able to work very hard, and" — "Well," she interrupted me, "what do you suppose Judge K. and Squire R. and Lawyer G. will say if you leave here?" "O, well, I shan't ask them," I replied, "to say anything about it. And by the way, I see you are in a jocular mood, and I am really glad to see you feeling so well. O, how I wish I could feel as happy and well myself. I hope, Lizzy, you will always enjoy yourself and never see such days and hours as I have." "But," said Miss Linn, "you generally seem light-hearted; yet I know the world does not seem always to go right with one; yet at other times the silver lining will make its appearance on the other side of every dark cloud." "But," said I, "when trouble comes without the least provocation on my part, it appears hard to become resigned; more so than it does when I have been in fault myself. This transitory silver cloud lining which you are so kind as to speak of, has sometimes given me comfort for a short time, and then the dark cloud appears again." "But it is not a good thing," said Miss Linn, to lay trouble to heart, but always look on the bright side of the picture?" "Yes, your counsel is good," I said, "but it is not always practicable. We can find silver spoons at the end of the rainbow, too; but when we get to where it appeared to be, it is just as far from you as it was before, and so we are lured on from one excitement to another, never coming to the end of the rainbow. Even riches do not satisfy the cravings of the human heart. The desires of the wealthy are not appeased, but they are forever grasping after bright objects in the future, so as to add something more beautiful to their treasury; add wealth to wealth, until their barns and storehouses are too small to contain their goods; and then they are not prepared to receive it. So the things that are wanted cannot be numbered."

CHAPTER XXVI.

The time had now arrived when I intended going to Nauvoo. So after spending a few weeks at my daughter's, I bid farewell to the loved ones to try my fortune, as I supposed, among strangers. The house and lot which I had bought several years before, I wished if possible to make my home. I had not heard anything in particular concerning the place since I left there with my two children. I had written to the recorder of deeds concerning my property, but could not learn that any deed had been placed on record except my own. However, my lot, with a number of others, had been vacated and thrown into an open field since the

Mormons left there, which had been fourteen years since; but I could not learn whether the buildings had been removed, or anything definite about it, only that no other deed had been recorded. On reaching there, I soon found that the place had gone out of my hands, and I could not prevail on the one who had the tax title to give me the chance of redeeming it, although he promised me something in the place of it, but afterwards refused to let me have a penny's worth of anything. This was a disappointment which I did not look for, and still I had no reason to look for anything else from such a man. It is true I had friends that would not see me suffer, and some who were once Mormons had remained there. Joseph Smith's wife was now an old lady, and was keeping a hotel, and several others who had been Mormons were now the old settlers of the place. I stayed with an old acquaintance during the first winter, and I must acknowledge I was not the happiest person in the world, for every attempt I made toward a living, or to bring about any purpose in regard to my welfare or prosperity, was sure to turn out a disappointment, and I became discouraged. The place had, since the Mormons left, been settled with a French community; after which the Germans came in and bought them out, and at the time of which I am writing there were but few French and fewer Mormons left in the place. I considered myself a stranger, without one whom I could substitute for those I had left. It is true I could see persons who once had been my acquaintances; but many years had made many changes in them.

The matter of dress was not considered expedient, therefore I could not expect much work in this line. My ambition, however, was not that of being idle; I was therefore prompted to commence some kind of work. The landlady of the mansion employed me to make a suit of clothes for her son; this was the first, after being settled in a little quiet home I called my own as long as I could pay the rent. But dark shadows hung over my head with no flattering interests, and all I had to encourage me was, I knew I could do almost any kind of work, and at a small price in this place, as people here were not in fact able to pay much for work. In this way I persevered for a number of months, having not enough to eat to be in the least degree half comfortable. My rent must be paid at all events, and my firewood cost me something, too, before it was prepared to use. I shall not go into the particulars of how much embarrassment I endured at this period, but will hasten onward to other events, one of which is that of teaching a small school. As soon as the district school was closed — it was now very warm, but as it was my fate to bear the burden and heat of the day, I fell victim to to this burden also — however, under existing circumstances I considered that I was somewhat favored in obtaining the school. My time and attention being fully occupied, I tried to make it enjoyable and pleasant. I had agreed to teach sixty days, but my marriage broke into this calculation; I only continued the school six weeks.

Now I had a home; but finding that my husbands means, or income, was not as I had anticipated, I in a short time began my accustomed occupation, the millinery business. Although he had dealt largely in merchandising in the east, and had bought this beautiful residence in this now quiet little city of Nauvoo, his income was not what I had supposed it to be. Nevertheless, willing heart and hands are what we need on such occasions, and I found myself possessed of both. Although my health or strength were not equal to the accomplishing of so much hard labor, yet I managed to the best advantage; and feeling also that it would be humiliating to surrender for the want of strength to accomplish and complete all in a respectable manner, I doubled every faculty in order to carry out my taste and purpose; and again, I did not intend to be superceded by any of my neighbors in housekeeping or any other domestic belongings. The work of millinery increased so that in a year or two I found it difficult to accommodate all who came with hats to reconstruct. This branch of the business was by far the hardest of any part, and I deemed it necessary to only attempt to have just enough, so that what was done should be neatly accomplished. My commendation depended upon the neatness of the work; also, having no assistance all was done by my own hands. On the first fourth of July I received over forty-two dollars in addition to what I had obtained for work the three months previous. It was now plain to me that the matter of dress was considered expedient, although it had been suggested to me differently at the commencement. My husband's two little girls now began to be a help in many respects. They were both very pretty; and this was not all, they were very good to me, which made me love them, although they were not my own. I now began to appreciate my expenses and hard labor about the place. It began to look more and more like home, for many changes had been made and it presented a different appearance.

I do not remember the number of inhabitants in Nauvoo at this time, but think it was about two thousand. The Temple had, four years previous to this been set on fire, and only one corner of the front was now remaining, and this was high, running up to a sharp point in such a manner as to render it unsafe for passers by. It originally was a large, spacious building in front, with large stone pillars and a steeple or turret very large and high, on which was engraved in large letters, "Holiness to the Lord." These letters were overlaid with gold; the year it was completed was also engraved in gold figures. The windows of the upright part were round, with painted glass, the colors red, white and blue; and running back from this was a part called the "Endowment room." This was also very large and long, but not as high as the other, with a flat roof and twenty-four windows. These could be moved off as desired, coming up to a point, with a ring in the top. After the finishing of the Temple, which was several years in building, it was very attractive. The man's head, and a hand holding a trumpet, were also a very great addition to the beauty of this magnificent structure. I visited this building with a number of other persons of my acquaintance and strangers who were almost constantly coming to see it and the city. The workmanship of the building was splendid. In the basement was a fountain with an oblong baptismal basin sculptured out, forming a complete baptismal fount, as it is called by the Mormon church. On each side of this basin of solid rock (this was large, and the water was conveyed either way through the bottom of the basin) there we e oxen of white lime stone, very natural, and twelve in number, all perfectly executed, so that the veins in the ears and nose were plainly seen. The horns were perfectly natural, with small wrinkles at the bottom. By these the fount was supported, and only the heads and fore shoulders were visible. We went into every part of the temple except in the endowment room. We were, however, on the top of that, and removed some of the windows and looked in, as we did not intend to leave the place until our curiosity was perfectly satisfied. It is impossible to describe all we saw, or to give a full description of the building. It was built by poor people, under the leadership of Joseph Smith, who said he was directed by revelations from God. The

Mormon church at this period may well be said to have been in its infancy; but at the time of which I am writing it was in ruins, and the Mormon church had nearly all emigrated fourteen years ago, and built up another city at Salt Lake.

In the year 1861 the civil war commenced, and my oldest son enlisted in the First Iowa cavalry. This news brought sadness to my stricken heart; but remonstrance on my part was of no avail. He was mustered into service in Davenport, after which he visited me at Nauvoo, and then joined his regiment in St. Louis. As they were stationed some time in Benton barracks I frequently received letters from him, and awaited with dread the time they should be ordered away. That would be the trying time with me. I acknowledge I was not in this respect very full of patriotic zeal; yet I felt this coming very near, for I had always depended on him for my support in my old age; and as things at this time presented rather an uncertain cast, I looked upon my son's enlisting in the army with feelings which I cannot describe. Golden fancies did not magnify realities in my condition, and my only hope depended on uncertainty; that is, if William should be killed or anything should happen to disable him, I should not know where to look for my maintenance, as for some time before his enlistment my health had been failing, and at that time I was unable to labor. My husband was aged and knew but little about managing with want or necessity. He never had labored for his living. As his father was wealthy and gave him a good start in the wholesale and retail merchandise, he was not prepared for toil, fatigue, hard labor or want. My youngest son had now enlisted also, and informed me that he would be transferred to the First Iowa light dragoons on arriving at St. Louis, and then they would serve in company L, under one command in an independent company, that is, being allowed to have their own horses.

There is One who knows the anguish of mind I was enduring at this time, and He is the only one who can know what thousands of mothers endured at this awful period. Being in constant expectation of the worst news that possibly could reach my hearing, I spent many long dreary nights in prayer and weeping. I have sometimes thought that if, in this life, we receive all the good or ill, and never have any part in any reward hereafter, how useless are our lives, and how unwise is our existence; but having a more sure promise, as the scripture says, " cast not away, therefore, your confidence, which hath great recompense of reward, for ye have need of patience; that after ye have done the will of God, ye may receive the promise" I felt the need of patience at this trying time, and also that I had a duty to perform. My husband's son was a lunatic, and also was afflicted with fits; and in a few years he became so troublesome we sent him to Jacksonville Insane Hospital. The sad burden was now removed, for a time, and the fear and dread also. My sons both came to visit me while on a furlough, but when the farewells were said, that was a time of weeping. My eldest daughter's husband had also enlisted in the army, and his regiment was ordered away to Pittsburgh Landing. He was in an engagement soon after they arrived at that place and was wounded and brought up to Keokuk, Iowa, with a boat load of wounded and sick soldiers. Every building which could be converted into a hospital was fitted up for the Iowa wounded soldiers, and filled. Keokuk is only twelve miles from Nauvoo, consequently we had an opportunity of visiting the hospitals whenever we were in the place. My son-in-law remained in the hospital three or four months almost entirely helpless, being wounded in the right hand, or wrist.

The small slivers of bones were working out daily, but he was considered highly favored, that it was no worse; as hundreds were dying daily in those hospitals, and it became a matter of little importance when a death occurred. I often received letters from my sons, and also money; and all through the war I was informed of all the proceedings of the first Iowa brigade, which was truly a great satisfaction. My daughter, who then lived in Keokuk, was also partaker with me in the hope that they would soon return to us safe and sound. My niece, who also lived in Keokuk, often visited me with words of comfort. She was an esteemable guest with us all — indeed Miss Wood's visits were looked forward to with great interest and anxiety. Being of a lively, cheerful disposition, her presence was a solace to every sorrow and care. Her words were fitly spoken, bringing life to a broken spirit. She seemed next to my own, in my heart's affections; and ever has had a place in my tender regards, as a faithful and living friend.

It was now autumn; the leaves on the trees were changing their color for a more rich hue, and the willows on the islands in the Mississippi were a yellowish red, and so compact that they resembled curling clouds at sunset; presenting a scenery most charming and beautiful. It was one of those days which makes one feel half joyful, half sad; and, forgetting one's self for a time, and also being beguiled by the beauties of nature, and forgetting (so to speak) even their own existence, and yet in silent meditations I thus wandered on, not knowing whither I was bound. Why was I left here to grope my way through this world alone? Why was my husband called away and I left here, only to be disappointed and decieved, and to meet with all the difficulty which human creatures are subject to or able to endure? I do not wish to stay where storms are awaiting me; no, I could not live always, and now on coming to myself, I was nearing the river bank and a short distance, a very short distance too, would have landed me twenty feet down a steep bank into deep water, (this bank had been washed under, in high freshets, leaving the surface very shallow, and the ground being sandy) I was at this time in a somewhat dangerous situation, and immediately turned my feet homeward to think no more of the past.

After receiving my supply of fall goods I commenced my usual business. My husband being well acquainted in that vicinity, assisted me in obtaining work, and I soon had a full supply; therefore my whole attention was taken up. The two little girls were adequate, for most of the work about the house, and this was a great relief. In again receiving letters from the war department, I learned that, instead of my sons coming home, they would be ordered away to Texas, under command of General Custer; that five Iowa regiments would be sent there as soon as the veteran infantry were discharged, as trouble was expected from Mexico. This news called for more patience on my part, but I found myself equal to this in a far greater degree than I had hitherto been. A little more and I should be as brave as any one could be. During their stay in Texas, after they had reached Galveston, I received letters from them as often as they could reasonably be expected to write; and I was informed of the transactions in that department while they remained there. In 1865, we were informed of President Lincoln's assassination. However slow the time appeared, the word came that the first Iowa cavalry were to be mustered out of service with several other regiments; and that was welcome news to me as it was to many others. My two sons and two sons-in-law reached home, and only one of them wounded and neither of them had been taken prisoners.

CHAPTER XXVII.

Soon after the closing of the war my oldest son rented a farm near Bellevue, after which he was married and removed to Sonora, Illinois. My youngest son remained near Bellevue for a number of years. Having thus far been so fortunate in having my greatest desire answered, I felt that if any one had reason to praise God it was myself. "We will rejoice in thy salvation, and in the name of our God we will set up our banners. The Lord fulfil all thy petitions."—Psalms, 20: 5.

Soon after I returned from a visit to Bellevue one of my neighbors inquired how I liked the place. Bellevue is a place, I am fully prepared to say, rather romantic in its appearance. Those high bluffs present a fanciful appearance for one thing; and again, the town is built in a place prepared for that purpose, a tract of land which is level running back from the river, forms a half circle, and high bluffs on either side. Within this half circle is a good mill site, formed entirely by enormous springs. In the center of this half circle there is an outlet, admitting of a road into the country; and above and below, on the river, are also roads leading into the country. It is also favored in a commercial view, first by water, second by railroad. I will relate a little adventure which happened while I was there at my son's. One fair, bright morning I started on a short walk. It was in the spring of the year; the birds were making joyous the air with resounding echoes of their happy mates, and all nature was awakened. Beauties were lavishly meted out in every direction, to amuse and stimulate us to action. My son had two hours before gone to his farm, and I concluded a little excursion around the bluffs to his place would be exhilarating. The distance was over a mile. I tripped on and enjoyed the morning walk very much as I hurried through the forest, and heard the woodland ring with the singing of beautiful feathered songsters. I now came to the farm, and after I had seen it and the prospects of farming, I was ready to bend steps homeward. My son directed a nearer route; I should go a little way up the bluff and I would find a foot path leading around it at the left. I commenced climbing. At first it was not very steep, and I expected soon to come to the path, but I found it was impossible. Being determined not to give up, I kept climbing until my feet was far above the tops of the highest trees, which grew highest on the bluff. It was now very steep and hard, so that nothing would grow, not a bush or shrub of any description to hold on to; and there was no such thing as turning to go down, so I kept on. If I had made any attempt to go down I should have fallen at least seventy feet before I could have been stopped by any tree or shrub, so my course was onward and upward. I had now got so high that I dared not look back, neither could I look to the right or left, and the little round stones were all I had to hold myself to the bluff; and sometimes these would come loose either in one hand or the other, and also under my feet. But now another obstacle came in my way; that was a ledge of rock. This parapet I considered impossible to surmount, but my only way was to try. The ground was so steep and slanting under my feet that I could not hang on only with my hands. There was no foothold in the rock, it being perfectly smooth all the way up. I knew a mighty struggle must be made, very soon, too; my strength began to fail, and I felt faint and sick. But suddenly my resolution returned; I prayed to God for strength and courage, for it was life or death; and this was quickly decided. I placed my hands firmly on the rock and pulled with a determination, and succeeded in pulling myself up, and then crawled on my hands and knees until I reached the top. I then sat down upon the brink of that horrible precipice, completely bewildered. My head swam, and for a time I was unconscious; but when I recovered I did not rise to my feet, for I was too near the brink, and my head was by no means regulated. It is still a mystery how I reached home. When my son came I was surprised to know it was noon, and my late adventure seemed like a dream, although it was a reality. My son declared, much as he needed money, he could not have been hired to go where I did for fifty dollars. "Only think," said he, "a woman of your age going where a strong man would not think of going for any small amount of money." "Well, say no more about it," said I; "I shall not try that over again."

I have often looked with admiration on those high bluffs along the Mississippi river; with feelings of great delight have I watched the birds flying around them where no man can climb. What a lovely place to build their nests and hatch their young. But now I can truly say they have no charms for me; I never could look upon a bluff again without a shudder.

I was now brought down again with illness. The fever, which had many times in my life brought me near the grave, had again come in a time when I was little prepared to meet its demands, and continued for some time. My husband's youngest daughter had gone to a high school in Ohio, and the oldest was married, and now we were alone; and as many things depended on my aid, it was a hard thing to surmount every difficulty. I had never heard from my friends in Salt Lake, except by a man from there who visited one of our neighbors. He informed me all he knew about them. However, his call had long since been forgotten when I received a letter from my first husband's niece. The letter read as follows:

"SALT LAKE CITY, April 3, 1870.

"DEAR AUNT:— We happened to hear about you, by one of our Mormon missionaries calling at your town, by the name of Lewis Robinson. Since he returned to Salt Lake, I have not seen him myself, so have not heard any particulars. He says you are keeping a millinery shop and doing well; that your children are all married. My children are all grown, but I don't think they ever will marry here. Uncle Ben came out here about two years ago. He is very much dissatisfied with this place, and talks of going back this summer. I should like to ask you a few questions about Mormonism there. Is it anything like it used to be in Joseph's day, or is it all a humbug like it is here? We hear strange stories. Mormonism out here is divided into several classes: the Brighamites, and the Godbeites, and the Josephites, and it puts one to their wits end to know which is right. We have been so terribly humbugged by Brigham, that I shall not be in any hurry to join another. There is a great commotion about the Cullens bill here. The women held a mass-meeting and passed resolutions, some of which would have made you laugh, should you have seen them. Then the men thought they would throw the women's calculations into the shade, and held another; but I think they will have their labor for their pains. We all want to go back there to settle, if its any healthier there than it used to be. Aunt will go back this spring if she can get her money. When you write, direct to Salt Lake City, Utah Territory. Respectfully,

"HORTENTIA HARTWELL."

My answer was as follows:

"DEAR NIECE:—I was happy to hear once more from you and yours, and happy to hear, by your most esteemed letter, the fact that you are convinced of the prodigality of Mormonism, and have come to the conclusion that it is all a humbug, and are now willing to return to a land of law, morality and the bible. I think the Mormons have all paid dear for the husks they have eaten, and have learned a lesson they never will forget. For my own part, I am thankful I was not one of the number who went to Salt Lake. Polygamy is one of the greatest curses that ever spit its poisonous venom into the hearts of any civilized community, doing a wrong which cannot be recalled; and I doubt if it can be ever pardoned. I am heartily sorry your parents were ever so zealous in a faith which has no foundation, but a quicksand muck, into which, if you step your foot, you sink deeper and deeper; and there is one thing which rejoices me, that is, that you have not been allured away into that horrible pit and mire, the measure of its depth no one knows, and the cast of its blackness is enough to startle any soul that ever had one thought of purity. Innocence is the happiness of the soul; once forfeited and lost, it will leave us forever and no repentance can recall it.

"Dear niece, I have spoken plain, but it is the truth, and I must tell you what I believe to be true, or not say anything in regard to it;

and as you have requested me to tell you how it is here, I have done so, freely and plainly. I must close. Hoping to hear from you again soon, I still remain your affectionate aunt,

"E. M. S."

This was the first and the only news I have ever received direct from Salt Lake; however, I have often heard from there, but it was indirect, and in the common news. My sister's little boy, who was left in my charge in Missouri, (after his mother's death) is now in Salt Lake and holds a high position. This vile doctrine has separated families and friends far apart, both in united relationship as well as in distance. It has destroyed the peace of happy, inoffensive neighborhoods, and seduced many a virtuous and respectable woman into vices from which there is no redemption.

CHAPTER XXVIII.

It was now getting late for millinery work to be called for; every one seemed to be supplied for the summer. I had accomplished a great deal of hard work at the straw refinishing during the hot weather. This kind of work must be done with speed and neatly executed, in order to make it a paying enterprise. It is also necessary that every part of it should be done so that it will bear the criticism of a skillful workman, and there is no other way to do this, in order to give satisfaction to your patrons and peace to one's self as when it is so respectably done that it commands silence on the part of the employer. However, as I have said before, my work was about done for the summer, and I was prepared to let the last jobs go whenever they were called for.

Just then I received a note from an old acquaintance, formerly from Espyville, Penn., requesting me to make her a visit at Fort Madison. This was a surprise, that one of my old classmates should be so near and yet so remote in my imagination. I could not treat her with indifference, that never would answer; and I soon made myself happy in her presence. This Mrs. Allen was a daughter of Mr. and Mrs. Espy, of Espyville, with whom I boarded in that place, and a good time was enjoyed by us. It had been a long separation, and the changes had been many both with Mrs. Allen and myself. Thomas Espy was practicing law in Fort Madison (this was a brother to the lady before mentioned). "We came out here," she said, "in '51; my husband bought a farm and paid one thousand dollars down, and agreed to pay the balance within the term of five years — at least so the notes ran — but within one year he was taken ill and died. It is seven years now, and nothing is paid yet; however, it is in my brother's care, but how it will turn I know not." "Well," said I, "it is in good hands, Mrs. Allen; your brother is a good man, he will do the fair thing by you and secure your land; and he is a successful lawyer, therefore you have nothing to fear in regard to this."

I now began to think about returning home; but Mrs. Allen would not listen to this. "We will visit the state's prison," she said, "and that will be something new. We will attend service at six o'clock Sabbath morning, and then we will see the convicts marched out. It will be splendid, indeed." "Yes," I replied, "I should be highly delighted to see them; I presume they are attended with good people." The best of associates is the company they keep, and no other. Their beautiful striped suits, too; how becoming. We attended the early services and saw eighty convicts marched into the large dining room, which was prepared for the purpose of holding the meeting. An excellent sermon was preached, and some of the prisoners joined in singing, and many of those unfortunate creatures showed deep emotion. The words of the text were selected by one of the prisoners. After services they were marched into their dark prison cells and the heavy iron doors were shut with a jarring, screeching noise, and the door was locked. " Now who knows but some of those poor prisoners are really — as some no doubt are — as clear from crime as those who visit those cells and are at liberty to go where they please," thought I. "'Tis not all who escape punishment that are deserving of liberty; and it is not all who are confined in prison cells who are not deserving liberty. And who knows but some of those are christians, being confined and yet approved of God; and having a conscience void of offence toward God and man, they can rejoice that they are counted worthy to suffer for Christ's sake, knowing also that nothing can separate them from the love of God." "Shall tribulation, or distress, or persecution, or famine, or nakedness, or peril, or sword, as it is written, for Thy sake we are killed all the day long; we are counted as sheep for the slaughter." "Nay, in all these things we are more than conquerors through Him that loved us; for I am persuaded that neither death nor life, nor angels, nor principalities, nor powers, nor things present, nor things to come, nor hight, nor depth, nor any other creature, shall be able to separate us from the love of God, which is in Christ Jesus, our Lord."

The next morning was clear and pleasant, and my mind was homeward; yet Mrs. Allen insisted on my remaining until we visited her brother, which I agreed to do that afternoon providing she would not detain me another day. This she agreed to. The visit being accomplished with much satisfaction and enjoyment, the following morning I took the train for home.

CHAPTER XXIX.

The summer grew warmer as the season advanced. Nothing of importance happened except the usual routine of summer life. The heat of the summer had now got to a great pitch; I never witnessed more intensity of heat since my remembrance, and I was seized again with fever. This was not an uncommon occurrence. This malady by which my father had several years before fallen a victim, was now preying upon my already wasted constitution, and for the next four months I knew but little of what passed. When I recovered I found it necessary to work in Fort Madison for at least one season of the millinery work, for reasons which I shall not name at present. Having become settled in a convenient place, and also having the assurance of having a full stock of millinery goods (which was according to agreement), to be supplied by one Mr. F. and his wife. The lady wished to learn the business of millinery, and agreed to furnish all the goods and give me half the profits for my work. This proved a failure, and non-performance of the agreement, and as fictitious as the initial of his name. However, I had agreed to take the house for a certain period, and expected to do as I agreed. But the only way which was sure, I could depend on myslef if all others failed. There was one thing I felt sure of, and that was a living, if no more; that was by hard work at the straw millinery.

I received a call one morning as I entered my shop; it was a young lady who wanted a situation with a milliner. She had worked at bleaching, and coloring and pressing; she also said she had goods and would bring them. This was what I so much needed, a good strong person to press hats, but I did not know as I could depend on her, I had been taken in so many times (she being a stranger) that now I did not know who to believe. This lady lived In Illinois, just over the river. I did not give her a decided answer, and she came to see me again the next week. I was at this time crowded with work, and must have help immediately; consequently I told her to come the next morning. When she came I did not notice any millinery goods; so this being a matter that did not concern me directly, I opened not my mouth until the next day or two; I then asked her if she brought any goods, or did she expect her goods sent to her on the ferry boat? "O, I have them with me," she said; and putting her hand in her pocket she took out a small parcel, and undoing it, "Yes, here is pretty near a yard of silk illusion and a little wire," she whined. "But where are your goods?" I asked, quietly, and at the same time feeling a little disgusted at her littleness. "This is all I have," she whined again. I almost fainted with sheer surprise. "You don't pretend to say that is millinery goods, do you?" "To be sure I do," she replied; ain't this millinery goods?" she said, holding up the strip of silk illusion. "I must confess I am surprised," I said, "but never mind, we will proceed with our work and let that go."

In a few days I received another call. A young lady wished a situation to learn bleaching, coloring and pressing hats, for which I should receive certain benefits. This proposal was agreed to, and she gave me ten dollars to seal the contract. The next week she came and told me she only wanted to stay one month; she would pay me for her board, and said she could learn in one month. I noticed a great difference in those two girls. One was stubborn and unyielding, morose and disagreeable, while the other showed a mild, pleasant, obliging disposition. One would judge them both very amiable, good dispositions, and worthy to be loved; but alas, the deception practiced by some no tongue can tell. Now as the month had passed, and my best girl had left me, well pleased and wholly satisfied that her time and money had been put to good use, Mary and I were left to argue and contend about this work not being done as it should be, or that lady was hard to please, or something of the kind. I many times thought they were easy to please if they would take the work she pronounced good. For my own part I should not accept it if it had been for me; however, I thought she would never have another opportunity of hurting my custom, and I rejoiced when she left my shop.

I still kept the place, and only visited my friends occasionally, for the reason that I could live there without having more to do than I was able to perform, on account of my ill health. I received a letter from my daughter, who lived in Kansas, requesting me to come to her; but the journey was long, it seemed like a long way to go, for me, at least, and I could not harbor the thought for a moment. My oldest son still lived in Sonora, Illinois, thirteen miles down the river below Fort Madison. The fall months were pleasant, the air mellow and fragrant with ripe fruit and autumn leaves. Nature itself had exhausted its powers and was now at rest; and the birds, after having a good supply out of God's full storehouse, could cease their warbling and fold their wings, and with their heads under their wings could rest without a thought or a care of to-morrow. The weather became a little more bracing and invigorating; the nights were cool and healthful, and poor weary mortals could find sweet repose when daily toil was done. At twilight, when the busy hours were over, and the hum of the work in the city was ended, this was a good time for silent meditation. I could then think over the past, and wonder at the goodness administered to me; that my life had been spared through so many dangers and my mind had still retained its reason. This has been a wonder many times, and is still a token of the unspeakable goodness of God. O, God, be thou my strong habitation whereunto I may continually resort. Thou hast given commandment to save me, for Thou art my rock and my fortress.

CHAPTER XXX.

Toward the last of December I fancied a visit to my son's would be quite pleasant, as the loneliness of my situation demanded something to cheer me. The distance, I imagined was not so far that I could not by any means whatever see him, and it was not impossible but I could get there. If I should start, probably after crossing the river I should fall in with a team passing that way; but after crossing the river I was disappointed not to see a ready opportunity, and walked on. The snow had began to melt fast, for the sun had taken a deep hold of the roads, and the water had already began to run in streams, which were over my rubbers. The river was one mile wide, and to return home would be to lose my journey thus far, and I continued on my way, but not rejoicing. At last a team came in sight; it was loaded with wood, and my chance for a convenient place to ride was rather slim. However, I made the best of a bad bargain, and for some time got along very well, until the going became so horrid it was not safe to go any farther, and I walked to Nauvoo that day. The next morning I labored hard to get to my son's, the distance being four miles. I could have walked that with less difficulty had it not been for my trip the day before. My son was not a little surprised to see me, and wondered at my undertaking such a trip. I told him he need not be in the least surprised, for this was a day of wonders and no one need be surprised at any occurrences whatever. The next morning the sun shone out bright and warm, reminding me of the danger in crossing over to Fort Madison again, which I intended to do. The next day the wind changed, blowing from the north. It had frozen considerable during the night, and on arriving at Fort Madison crossing, we were told it was not safe for teams on the ice, and they doubted its being safe for one person to cross alone, as the river was rising very fast, and a part of the old ice had sunk, and the only chance of getting over would be on the thin scale which had frozen since the wind changed to the north. I do not know the thickness of the ice; however, I ventured to go alone, but had not proceeded over three or four rods before the ice began to sink and I stepped lightly back to the shore. Just then I observed two men coming down to the river. They beckoned me to come that way and I immediately went to them. "I expected to see you break through the ice," said one, and continued, "now if you will follow me, I think I can pilot you over." "You are very kind," said I; "but probably when we reach the second island I will be safe to try getting over alone." "I do not know how that is," said my friend, "we can tell better when we get there." We hurried on until we came to the first island: the ice sank a little every step, and as we advanced it became worse and more dangerous; the old ice had sunk just enough to allow the current through between the old and the new ice, and this caused a kind of groaning, melancholy sound, and as near as I can conceive the noise resembled unhappy spirits in torment. We came to a broken place; it was the steamboat channel, and this was fathomless. The water was pouring, foaming, and dashing through this channel with such fury, and a groaning noise, that I thought and said it was impossible to get over; still my friend told me 'twas not safe to stand one minute on the ice; we had nothing to help ourselves, neither rope nor pole, and depended entirely on Providence. In much less time than it takes to tell this, my escort had leaped over and reached me his hand. I could not get a very firm grasp, the distance was so far, but gave a desperate spring and my feet just cleared the edge of the ice. Thinking this was the only place we would have to cross, we hurried on to the second island. The going was more difficult owing to the sharp, freezing cold wind, and a light snow. This made it very slippery walking as well as the momentary danger of falling through the ice. After crossing the second island just at the edge of the land, there was another broken place, worse than the first; and now what way to manage to cross? This was perfectly awful. The cold wind had so chilled me, I was thinking I should not be able to hold out much longer at the best; however, twenty minutes would decide the case; it would be either life or death. My companion leaped over and reached me his hand. At first I could not get anywhere near touching his hand, but coming as close to the edge as I possibly could, and reaching as far as I could, he pulled me over this horrible place also. I was very thankful that we had thus far escaped the danger. We passed on without knowing what danger awaited us before reaching the opposite side of the river. We now were half way over, and the most dangerous part was before us; this was the main body of the river. The current was washing under the thin scale of glassy ice, and as we passed along the rocking, tetering road, and heard the water gurgling and groaning just under our feet, it made me shudder to think of the danger which lay in our path, and from which there was no escape. However, we were within hailing distance of Fort Madison, and as we came nearer we came to another broken place, but this was soon remedied. Those on shore ran with a plank, and I was safe!

The remaining part of winter passed pleasantly, and beautiful spring appeared, dressed in green, smiling at the singing of birds and the thought of the rose wreathed-mantle which Dame Nature was weaving for her graceful shoulders. I have often thought, while gazing upon those beautiful wild rose wreaths, climbing along the thick shelving green lamina-like groves, or wild woodland, and presenting an appearance which reminds one of sweet Heaven where roses are without thorns, and have often thought I should see them depicted in that happy abode, which is prepared for those who are faithful.

The summer was magnificent which invites the human family to come forth, to inhale the life-giving atmosphere. This was a luxury of which many availed themselves, and the appreciation of the splendid summer was shown by the numerous representatives. In every direction men, women and children were seen strolling along the river bank, or sailing in boats, or wandering in meadows, or green pastures, or in gardens or bowers; all seemed to love the fresh, bracing, invigorating, loving atmosphere. My time had been vigorously occupied during the summer months, with my usual avocation. It was now September, and as I promised myself a visit to Kansas this pleasant fall, preparations were made accordingly. In October I made this promise good. Arriving at Atchison I was surprised to see so large a city, and, as we passed along, the farms and all improvements showed thrift and enterprise. Two day's travel brought me to Burlingame, Osage county and at the conclusion of my journey, the country presented a pleasing view. The rolling prairie, the clear and living brooks, the groves of wild plums and forest trees interspersed, dotting the land with nature's own bowery; the lowing of fat cattle, having a bountiful supply of free range, wallowing in luxurious abundance; this, with many other benefits by no means trifling, surrounded and filled the state of Kansas.

I was now at my daughter's, and surrounded with smiling faces and cheerful hearts and hands. Sarah and William Montgomery were the owners of a farm five miles from Burlingame. The prospect around them looked favorable in many respects. My son-in-law had settled there soon after the war, and had struggled hard to make a beginning, and which had succeeded; and now the prospect was a well to do future. At this period, the roads were thronged with emigrants. The first winter the house was filled with movers who could get no further on account of the cold and snow; and sometimes would remain two weeks or more. Mr. Montgomery was a man who never could say "no," or "I don't know;" he always said "yes, stay and welcome, as long as you can make yourselves comfortable." I thought sometimes they put too long a meaning to his words, and stayed longer than any of us could be comfortable; for the noise of children completely drowned every word spoken in the house; and it appeared to me I should soon be a fit subject for the insane asylum. "It is a satisfaction, notwithstanding, to know that the winter will not continue long," I said to my daughter as the house became clear from emigrants. "Yes, but it will last two or three months longer," said Sarah, "they have commenced coming early, they all seem to know where they can stop, and stay, too. Hundred and Ten Creek seems to be known by all who come this way; what a bother!"

Spring at last came, the snow and ice disappeared, and the green grass was spread over the vast rolling prairie. I think of all seasons of the year, springtime is the most exhilarating. I love the spring for its flowers and birds, its green herbage, its fresh soft air; for its season to work, for business of all kinds, for stir and enterprise in labor both domestic and mental. As the season advanced emigration became abundant, long strings of covered wagons could be seen as far as the eye could reach. Some of the emigrants we found, as they camped at Hundred and Ten Creek, were in want of provisions, while others were abundantly supplied with all things. necessary for they journey. This travel was continued until the grasshopper famine which brought much suffering. The travel was then discontinued and almost all business suspended.

At this period I was engaged in a millinery room in the village of Burlingame, but the famine plainly indicated to me what my prospect would be in the future. The relief committee distributed aid among that class of sufferers who had families of children. Farmers who but a few days ago had proudly examined their bountiful fields and returned with faces beaming with delight, thrift, and a gladsome harvest in their imagination, now walked out only to see the destroyer's handiwork accomplished in one day's time, and returned with arms folded, and on their countenances was the picture of starvation. The change was wonderful. It was now apparent that a change must ensue with me. In my circumstances I could not remain where people were not able to furnish sufficient patronage for my support. Some farmers were profane in their expressions concerning the grasshoppers; others seemed more thoughtful. Some were leaving their farms and going to their friends in the east; that, however, was not a general thing, as but few could leave all. "The scourge grows worse every year," said one man to his nieghbor. "The ground is full of grasshopper eggs and there's no getting rid of them." "My friend, said the other, "did you ever read what Christ said? 'ask, and ye shall receive; seek and ye shall find; knock, and it shall be opened unto you.' Now, I think if we turn our attention to God, and give more heed to the welfare of our souls, and not care so much about the things of this life, it would be better for us.

God designs that we shall trust in Him and look to Him for our daily bread; and after we have done all we can and continue to do all in our power to His honor and glory and feel resigned to His dealings toward us, we will find He is not slack concerning His promises."
"Yes," said the first, "I know all about that. I thought once I was a Christian; but since I came to Kansas, somehow or other, things have gone against me; and I know I have not felt as thankful as I used to feel for His favors. In fact, I have thought but little about it. I came out here for the purpose of getting something ahead, but I have come to nothing now."
"Yes, I see how it is," said the other, "'he that seeks to save his life, shall loose it; and he that seeks to loose his life, for My sake, shall find it.' The cares of this life choke the good seed that was sown in our hearts, and bring no fruit to perfection; so it's no wonder the fruit of our fields are cut off and our prospects are barren also. When I read what great and mighty works have been done through prayer and faith toward God, 'by faith kingdoms have been subdued, righteousness wrought, promises obtained, the mouths of lions stopped, the violence of fire quenched, the edge of the sword escaped; and out of weakness men have been made

strong, and waxed valiant in fight, turning to flight the armies of the aliens, all of these things have deen done through faith,' I am ashamed of myself as a professor of Christianity." "So am I," said the other, "and hope for the future to live more as God designed. I see now that I have missed a great deal of good. Let me live (hereafter) the life of the righteous, that my last days may be like theirs; and those little hinderances, let us pass them by, for the scripture tells us that if we endure chastisement, 'God dealeth with us as with sons; for what son is he whom the father chastiseth not, for if ye be without chastisement, then are ye bastards and not sons.'"

I many times saw what I never expected to see — that is want of something to eat, and no possible way of getting one mouthful. Yet I considered myself better off than many others. I made no application for help, knowing there were others who needed all they could get to keep their little ones from starvation. In the month of November I bid my children in Kansas farewell. Mrs. Friend, the pastor's wife, and Mrs. Judge Billings, accompanied me to the depot; they also bestowed many little comforts necessary for my journey. The train came, and I left their smiling faces to meet again where the parting kiss will never be on our lips, and "good bye" will never be repeated. I was now leaving the associations which twined around my heart — my children, my christian friends and the church. The scenes were different and changeable, although it offered time for meditation. I also found that many were leaving Kansas on account of the grasshopper famine. The first night on the road I observed a lady dressed in deep mourning, who had four little children; and thinking she had probably just lost her husband, and her seat being next to mine, I inquired if her home was in Kansas. "No, I have been living in Mexico," she said. "Is your husband living?" I inquired. "No, he was killed in Mexico about two months ago. He was a cattle dealer; he was shot off his horse by one of his men. Those Mexicans are rough; it's nothing for them to shoot a man; it is a common occurrence there. I had no relatives in that country, and sold my property for about half its value, and am going to my father's, in Illinois." "I can in a small measure sympathize with you," I said. "I came to Kansas to visit my daughter, and while there my son wrote of my husband's death. I intended to make Kansas my home after this news, but the grasshopper famine came, and that put an end to this calculation. My daughter had written to me to come to Madison, Wisconsin, some time ago, but thinking probably times would be better, I remained another year, and finding it still more difficult to live, I abandoned all hope of remaining where peaple were not able to give me employment." I then said, "It is a good thing to know of one who knows all our troubles, one in whom we can confide all our sorrows; the only one who can fully satisfy and comfort us in our afflictions." "Probably that is the case," she said; "religion is something I know nothing about; my husband was a man of the world, and riches was all we cared about." "Don't you think it would have been better," I asked, "if you had sought the kingdom of Christ and tried to live christians?" "Perhaps it would," she said, "but I don't know." "Do you ever read the bible?" I inquired. "No, I have not lately, or since I left my home; I mean my father's," she replied. "Now let me tell you one thing," I continued, "if you will turn your attention to this subject, and pray for His holy spirit to direct you in wisdom's ways, you will soon say the half had not been told you. The enjoyment of the religion of Christ is the greatest enjoyment which possibly can be obtained in this life; and if we neglect this we are depriving ourselves of the greatest happiness that can be enjoyed." The passengers had gathered around to hear the conversation, and some of them finally got into an argument, and I said no more on that subject.

It now began to show daylight in the east, and glad was I that one night more would end the journey. We crossed the Mississippi river at daylight, and the next morning at four o'clock we arrived at Madison. After a visit to my daughter's, for the period of two months, I then received an answer to a letter from my sister in Fond du Lac, requesting me to visit her, as it was uncertain if I would ever have another chance to see her in this life. My sister, Mrs. Hulce, had at this time been under the care of a skillful physician for some time, and now every hour of delay admonished me of the danger of being too late, as the best of medical aid did not have any effect. I therefore hastened to her. I found her better; but the change which time had made was striking; and her appearance indicated that her time with us had almost expired. Although she revived for a short period, she again grew weaker and weaker, and finally fell to sleep, being fully prepared for the Master's use.

> Hark, a voice divides the sky;
> Happy are the faithful dead,
> In the Lord who sweetly die;
> Them the Spirit hath declared
> Blest, unutterably blest.
> Jesus is their great reward;
> Jesus is their endless rest.

My beloved sister Jane had also left me. One after another were dropping into the tomb, and I am left to spend a few more days of loneliness, then if I am faithful I shall meet them in a happier world, where all will be perfectness and love. May God in His goodness grant that we may all meet in a far better and brighter world, where "farewell" is never a cause of tears, but where peace and joy unspeakable fills every heart. Parents and children will greet each other there, when all worldly objects are past, and all temptations overcome through the power of faith in Christ; and where all sinfulness and care, adversity and hardships and toil, will forever pass from our memory. How easy our Savior has made it for us to come to Him. We are not worthy, but He is worthy. We are sinful, but He is holy and pure and righteous, and through His worthiness we can come and He will save us. If we are ever so poor we can come to Him just as well as though we possessed thousands; and if we are ever so much despised and low in the eyes of the world, he will receive us just as well as though we were kings or queens. He says He will prepare a place for us, and where He is there we can be also. O, what a beautiful place it must be, prepared by the Savior; one who has laid down His life for our salvation. O, why are we so careless? Had we not better serve Him with good, honest hearts? Since our blessed Savior has done so much for us, can we do too much for Him?

> "Ashamed of Jesus, that dear friend,
> On whom my hopes of heaven depend?
> No, when I blush be this my shame,
> That I no more adore His name.
> Ashamed of Jesus? yes I may,
> When I've no guilt to wash away;
> No tear to wipe, no good to crave,
> No fear to quell, no soul to save.
> 'Till then, nor is my boasting vain;
> 'Till then I boast a Savior slain;
> And O, may this my glory be,
> That Christ is not ashamed of me.

When I look over the scenes of my past life and the life which is to come, my hope within the vale is like an anchor to the soul. I can rest with the assurance that I have chosen a safe foundation for my hopes of happiness here, and in that glorious mansion, life everlasting.

I should be afraid to venture my eternal all on any other foundation than the one which is laid down in the bible as to the plan of salvation. All worldly reason is but mockery — a dazzling of the scenes, if it mistakes the decisive points of the plan of salvation. There is nothing important in life but this single object; all the rest is a dream, in which any mistake is of little importance. Trust not yourselves, therefore to the multitude which is of the party who err. Take not as guides those who can never be your sureties; leave nothing to chance or to the uncertainty of events, it is the hight of folly, where eternity is concerned. There is an infinity of paths which appear right to many; yet nevertheless they lead to endless death. Almost all who perish, do it in the belief that they are in the way to everlasting life, and all reprobates will be surprised when they hear the sentence, because they expected the inheritance of the just.

We must undergo the moulding and shaping into whatever form our good Master designs, and if we cannot endure to be moulded and refined as clay in the potter's hands, or as gold in the furnace, we are not fit for the Master's use. If I have suffered for the Kingdom of God, happy am I; glory to His holy name. And O, if I could be counted worthy to be one of that number who came out of great tribulation, having my robe washed white in the blood of the lamb, and be permitted to stand with those who have suffered before His throne and serve Him day and night in His temple! "He that sitteth on the throne shall dwell with them; they shall hunger no more, neither shall they thirst any more; neither shall the sun light on them, nor any heat, for the Lamb which is in the midst of the throne shall feed them, and shall lead them unto living fountains of water; and God shall wipe away all tears from their eyes." It is now over forty years since God, for Christ's sake, forgave my sins; since that time I have the assurance that if anything was lacking, or any hindrance which kept me from the comfort of His love in my heart, it was my own fault. He has always been ready to receive me back whenever I came to Him. This has taught me my dependence on Him every moment, and a continual watchfulness. I therefore find it a very great thing to live a divine life. We have a work to perform; something to do; and in order to do this work we must not trust to our own strength, we must keep our hand in His. "He that overcometh the same shall be clothed in white raiment; and I will not blot out his name out of the book of life, but will confess his name before my father and before his angels."

What eye, save one, seeth in secret; notices the human heart enjoying fellowship with God? What ear, save the one that heareth every sigh, is open to listen in those moments of soul repentings and deep sorrowings for its follies, mistakes and sins? There are seasons of soul elevation, when the sincere walk softly before God, with prayers and tears, which flow inwardly, cleansing the soul of pollution, unseen, unheard by friend or neighbor, but seen and heard by Him who keeps "the book of remembrance." "They shall be mine, saith the Lord of hosts, when I come to make up my jewels."

CHRISTIAN AT WORK.

"What is your secret?" asked a lady of Turner, the great painter. "I have no secret, madam, but hard work." "The difference," says Dr. Arnold, "between one man and another, is not so much in talent as in energy." It was a saying of Sir Joshua Reynolds, that "nothing is denied well directed labor, and nothing is to be attained without it." "Excellence," says Dr. Johnson, "can now be obtained by by the labor of lifetime; but it is not to be purchased at a lesser price." Says Sidney

Smith, "There is but one method, and that is hard labor; for distinction had better at once dedicate himself to the pursuit of the fox." There is a French proverb which reads, "step by step, one goes very far." It is a well known saying of Mirabeau, that "Nothing is impossible to a man who can will. This is the only law of success." "Have you ever entered a cottage, ever traveled in a coach, ever talked with a peasant in the field, or loitered with a mechanic at the loom," asked Sir Edward B. Lytton, "and not found that each of these men had a talent you had not; knew something you knew not?" Work, constant, honest, well directed work; that is the royal road to permanent distinction, to lasting success; and there is no man, however moderate his mental endowments may be, who may not by faithful work, give the world something which it never would have had without him.

CHAPTER XXXI.

There is one more clause concerning the government and rules of the Mormon church; that is this: All members, according to their law, are strictly forbidden to speak one slanderous word against his neighbor. This is in their book of commandments by which the church is governed. It reads thus: "Cease to speak evil one of another; cease to be idle, for the idler shall not eat the bread nor wear the garment of labor; cease to eat meat; and again, hot drinks are not good for man, neither strong drink, which is not good for man nor beasts; cease to do evil and learn to do well; and again, cleanliness is commendable, and next to godliness." These rules are, or were, strictly adhered to while we remained among the Mormons. I do not know what has been their creed since their removal to Salt Lake, as I never visited that place.

IMMORALITY AND THE DRUNKARD.

Those two evils always go hand in hand. They are twin brothers. What one suggests, the other readily agrees to. They are always good friends, and never disagree except when "Drunk falls into the ditch." "Immorality" never lends him a helping hand, for this is against his principles. The drunkard, therefore, wallows in the mire until the aid of Sobriety or Morality is obtained, and then "Immorality" folds his arms and looks on, until he is able to walk again. Then "Immorality takes him by the hand and they travel on, good friends as ever. My erring friends, this is what Temperance is doing for you; will you be helped out of the mire?

LITTLE CHILDREN.

My dear little friends: I wish to say a few words to you before I close this book, and will say as good things as I can think of, and that you will find in the bible, that teaches us all how to be good. Did you ever read where it says: "Children, obey your parents in the Lord, for this is right." And then it says: "Honor thy father and thy mother," which is the first commandment, with promise that it may be well with thee, and that thou mayest live long on the earth. You all would rather live than to die and leave your parents, and brothers and sisters, and schoolmates. If so, you have the promise of living if you keep this commandment. In the First Book of John, in the beginning of the second chapter, it says: "Little children, these things write I unto you, that ye sin not." And also the 28th verse: "And now, little children, abide in Him, that when He shall appear we may have confidence, and not be ashamed before Him at His coming." And again he says, in the third chapter, seventh verse: "Let no man deceive you. He that doeth righteousness is righteous, even as he is righteous." And in the second chapter, 12th verse, he says: "I write unto you little children because your sins are forgiven you for His name's sake." We read that Jesus called little children to him and said: "Suffer little children to come unto me, and forbid them not, for of such is the kingdom of heaven." The bible tells a great deal more about little children; you must find all you can that it says about you, for then you will know how to act, and how to be good children; and then when you are men and women you will be respected and loved by everybody. Will you try?

THE YOUTH.

I have a word to say to my youthful friends. My hearty wishes and desires could not be at peace without a little friendly advice. I will say, in the first place, I have been young, therefore I know the besetments which lurk in the path of the youth. That is the time which is the most dangerous period of their life, and that is the time they need counsel; but, alas! how few accept it, even from their best friends. You will find good counsel in the Book of Proverbs, which says: "My son, forget not my law, but let thy heart keep my commandments; for length of days, and long life, and peace, shall they add to them; let not mercy and truth forsake thee; bind them about thy neck; write them upon the table of thine heart; so shalt thou find favor and good understanding in the sight of God and man. Trust in the Lord with all thine heart, and lean not unto thine own understanding; in all thy ways acknowledge Him, and He shall direct thy paths; be not wise in thine own eyes; fear the Lord and depart from evil."

These are the words of a wise man, and happy would those be who follow his counsel. If you should obey your parents you need not disobey any of those valuable sayings; for no good person will advise their children to act unwisely. The fourth chapter of Proverbs says: "Hear ye, children, the instruction of a father, and attend to know understandingly; for

I give you good doctrine; forsake ye not my law. Happy is the man that findeth wisdom, and the man that getteth understanding, for the merchandise of it is better than the merchandise of silver, and the gain thereof than fine gold. Wisdom is more precious than rubies; and all the things thou canst desire are not to be compared to her." We read that the "fear of God is the beginning of wisdom."

THE MORMON TEMPLE.

The temple at Nauvoo, Illinois, was built by tithing. It was the custom, or the law of the Mormon church to receive the tenth part of what each member possessed. If there were members who did not own property, they were expected to work on some public building or public improvement, one tenth part of his or her time. The ladies paid their tithing by making carpets; or, if skilled, in making saleable embroaidery, or bedspreads, or quilts, or clothing, or hosiery, or any fancy saleable work which could be turned into money, by a committee chosen for that purpose, and appropriated for the good of the church, in buildings or improvements, to increase and enrich the value of the church at large.

MY BROTHER'S DEATH.

I have just received news of my oldest brother's death, with whom I resided when Mormonism first made its appearance, and with whom I conversed in the grove at the time Mr. Sherer held my hand, and who was one of those who signed the copy of complaint entered against me by the Presbyterian church in Sandford, New York. All of those concerned in this affair, have now left the theater of earth; and, like the messenger sent to Job, I alone am escaped to tell the story.

THE DANITES.

Some of the truths herein disclosed may bring some to wonder that any should be so well versed in the theorem of those secret bands of prowling Danites, who are traveling through the country under the name of tramps. This country has for many years past been filled with an unusual flood of burglars. It may be already understood that many evil-designing persons have united with the Mormon church for the purpose of having a shelter for their crimes; knowing at the same time that the Mormons would have to bear the name, also the blame, of their evil deeds.

It has now been many years since I was so fortunate as to make my escape from that class of people; and hoping this will be a warning to others, I feel it my duty to explain those things; and, of a truth, will further say that they are unlike what they appeared to be in the commencement. I now look back with astonishment, that so many well-meaning people, also those of high respectability, and even distinction in good moral and religious society, have, unfortunately, been drawn into their unobserved coils.

The order, or practice of healing the sick among the Mormons, is the laying on of hands; therefore, if any are sick among them, they call on the Elders of the church, two or more; and, as they say, the prayer of faith shall save the sick; and if they have committed sin, it shall be forgiven them. The order, also, of baptizing for any sickness, is considered essential to health; however in this case, they also perform the same ceremony as for converts. They are also baptized for their dead friends, vicariously taking upon themselves the name of the deceased friend, those who have died without being baptized; as they say, "thus bringing them into the kingdom of God."

Speaking in tongues is also praticed among

the so-called Saints, and the interpretation of tongues. Order, in all business concerns, is truly a marked feature among them in all pursuits of life.

I have, in relation to what I have written concerning the Mormons, given an accurate account of all events which have occurred within my own knowledge; and have relied on the principle, "to prove all things and hold fast to that which is good."